MW00946370

Cooking for a Longer, Healthier Life

Carico, Helping People to Live a Longer Healthier Life

Food Editor: Lois Smith
Cover Design: Shawn Pierce

ISBN-13: 978-1537185774
ISBN-10: 1537185772

DEDICATION

Reducing the risk of disease, increasing energy, and improving our immune systems. *"The great law of Life is Replenishment. If we do not eat, we die. Just as surely, if we do not eat the kind of food which will nourish our body constructively, we not only die prematurely, but we suffer along the way."*

Dr. Norman Walker (lived to 99 years)

CONTENTS

PREFACE

Since starting Carico International in 1967, I had the realization that there were five distinct areas of life people could improve upon to help achieve a healthy lifestyle. The proper selection and preparation of the food we eat, the quality of the air we breathe, the value of a good night's sleep and an exercise program are extremely important to ensure that you and your family will enjoy a much healthier lifestyle. For over the last 50 years it has been my passion to develop the finest product lines in the world to help you accomplish your health and longevity goals. Today, more than ever before, it is important that we focus on prevention, rather than cure.

Most people realize that the selection of food is extremely important for maintaining good health, but how we prepare the food determines the nutritive value we receive from the foods we eat. The Carico method of food preparation will help you obtain the maximum nutritional value in the food you cook.

Everyone realizes that water is a vital part of good health, as water makes up 75% of our body. The quality and quantity of the water we drink is an important factor in our family's health. Carico's water purifier will remove 99% of all contaminants, while retaining the mineral content so important for your health.

Today, people are much more aware that the air we breathe can contain many contaminants, off-gassing and dangerous particles that can have a serious impact on our health. This unhealthy air may cause asthma, allergies and other respiratory problems. By utilizing Carico's air purification system, you can avoid breathing many of the contaminants and dangerous chemicals that exist throughout your homes and offices, thus creating a fresh, safe breathing environment for you and your family.

One of the most important factors in regenerating our bodies is deep, restful sleep. The Carico Silver Collection Sleep System is the only mattress in the world that can ground you like Mother Nature intended by creating the same effect as sleeping on the beach and touching the ground. The more you learn about grounding, the more you will appreciate this revolutionary patented product.

And last, but not least, it almost goes without saying that we all need regular exercise. Good exercise helps avoid many long-term health problems such as heart disease, high blood pressure, circulation issues and obesity.

By focusing on these five areas, you and your family can be assured of enjoying a longer and healthier life.

And now, I hope you enjoy and use the recipes and knowledge in this book to help you live a longer and healthier life.

To your health and wellbeing,

Richard R. Cappadona

Richard R. Cappadona
Founder and President, Carico International

FORWARD
Chef Charles Knight

Now that you've invested in a set of Carico Ultra Tech II™ cookware, it's time to reap the many rewards of hassle-free cooking, delicious meals and improved health. I know through my years in the culinary and cookware business that nothing detracts more from a pleasurable cooking experience than not having the right equipment to work with.

As an accomplished home cook and chef, I want my finished dishes to appeal to the eye and the palate, and to meet my family's nutritional needs. Overcooked vegetables that have lost their color and flavor have little nutritional value. Dried out, tasteless cuts of meat are difficult to chew and swallow. With the Ultra Tech II™ Cooking System, you can rest assured that these cooking nightmares won't happen to you. Waterless/Greaseless cooking retains valuable vitamins, minerals and taste, as well as the natural moisture in your foods.

Because we understand your lifestyle needs, much care went into the selection of the recipes in this cookbook. In addition to including the most nutritious entrees, Carico has made your variety of choice almost limitless. Choose from irresistible recipes, such as Turkey Stuffed Peppers, Eggplant Parmigiana or Meatloaf, and even Angel Food Cake and Marbled Brownies.

Part of my role as a culinary consultant has been healthy meal development and determining the nutritional information for each recipe. Through this process, I've listed, tasted and visualized each meal personally. To prepare healthier meals each recipe went through a number of testing stages to reduce fat, sodium and calories. Each recipe was then retested for taste, quality and accurate preparation instructions.

So much has been written about nutrition, cholesterol, fats and diets during the past thirty years, it's no wonder we sometimes feel confused by all the information. That's why in this cookbook we've gotten back to the basics of *Cooking for a Longer, Healthier Life*

I've known Rick Cappadona and the people of Carico for nearly five decades and have enjoyed their high quality products, especially my Ultra-Tech II™ cookware. You will too! Easily prepared, nutritional meals that are appealing to the eye and the palate… What more could you ask for?

CHAPTER 1

Health... Our Most Important Asset

The answer to better health is exercise and the food we eat. Nutritious, low-fat, low-sodium meals reduce dangerous cholesterol, cut unwanted calories and retain important minerals, vitamins and life giving enzymes. All of our fresh foods have a built-in, natural goodness. But the wonderful, health-giving values you paid dearly for at your grocery store may soon disappear in your kitchen. With old-fashioned conventional cooking methods, fresh vegetables must be peeled, boiled or steamed, and subjected to the high heat of a microwave, not to mention the use of cooking fats and oils. All of this results in the irreplaceable loss of a large share of the vital minerals, vitamins and enzymes that we need for better health.

Eating a variety of fresh fruits and vegetables is sound advice from the American Cancer Society for cancer proofing your diet. Additionally, most experts recommend cutting down on fats and eating healthy amounts of fiber, the same prescription the American Heart Association recommends to reduce the risk of heart disease. Maintaining the natural goodness in your foods is the focus of *Cooking for a Longer, Healthier Life.*

Ultra-Tech II™ waterless, greaseless cookware creates wholesome, great tasting meals, without sacrificing vitamins, minerals and enzymes. Furthermore, the cooking methods you will learn thoroughly capture the wonderful flavors we expect in our meals. It's possible because of this unique cooking method. Foods are cooked at precise temperatures, below the boiling point, in a vapor seal. This Ultra-Seal™ method of waterless cooking with Ultra-Tech II™ cookware is the secret that retains vital nutritional values. By eliminating the need for peeling, boiling, steaming and microwaving, vegetables and fruits come to the table with a "garden fresh" taste, and meats are gently browned and cooked in their own natural juices, without the need for high calorie oils and fat. It's a whole new experience in cooking and taste, and a key benefit for better health.

Because food preparation is easy and efficient, waterless cooking with Ultra-Tech II™ cookware has become the preferred method of preparing meals for millions of home cooks and professional chefs who are dedicated to better health through healthier cooking techniques. *Cooking for a Longer, Healthier Life* contains exciting recipes that will bring nature's goodness to your table every day.

There are two fundamental guidelines that we always include in our cookbooks. First, the recipes must be quick and easy to prepare, with ingredients that are readily available. And second, every recipe must be tasty and healthful.

What are Today's Cooking Options?

Aluminum: (Anodized and Non-Anodized): Stains, warps and dents easily. Chemically reacts with food. Harsh chemicals and scrubbing pads can erode the coating. Metal handles get hot and it's difficult to clean.

Coated finish: Costly to replace year after year. During the cooking process, the coating chips off and contaminates the food you eat. Overheated, nonstick pans emit harmful VOC's, a toxic mixture of chemicals that may be harmful to your health.

Enameled Steel: Chips, cracks and stains. Food eventually sticks and burns.

Cast Iron: Heavy, porous, rusts when cleaned with soap and water. When the pan gets hot the metal expands, opening pores that absorb food. When cooled, the food is retained in those pores and released when heated again. Unhealthy.

Microwaving: Convenient, but extreme heat degrades the quality, taste and nutritional value of food, causing it to become tough and unappealing in color and texture. Microwaving with plastic containers may leach chemicals into the food, causing a change in the food's molecular structure. Is this unhealthy cooking convenience worth compromising your health?

What is the Solution?

Ultra-Tech II™ Cooking System. The finest food preparation system in the world. Designed to cook vegetables without high heat, boiling or steaming, while preserving nutrition, taste and color. Meat, poultry and fish cook without oil or fat. *Carico, Helping People Live a Longer, Healthier Life!* Here's how it works. It starts with…

9 Layers of Perfect Ultra-Core Plus™ Design

The luxurious, polished exterior exudes an enduring, easy-care beauty that lasts and lasts. The high-grade surgical stainless steel interior resists staining, is easy to clean, and there is no chemical reaction with the food cooked. The high-impact bonded base is warp resistant, providing superior heat conduction and maximum contact with the cooking surface. No need to use high heat. ***Medium to Low Heat is all you Need to Know.***

Double Thermal Core Construction. A perfect blend of metals and alloys. Heat is quickly distributed from the bottom up, the sides in and across the cover. It's the best heat-conducting pan ever!

- **Layer 1: 304 Surgical Stainless Steel (inside)** – The most sanitary metal to come in contact with your food. Sunburst finish is easy to clean. No coating to come off in your food. Easy to clean!

- **Layer 2: Surgical Stainless Steel (outside)** – Mirror finish, long lasting, easy to clean and induction compatible.

- **Layers 3 thru 5: Thermal Core** – Aluminum alloy, pure aluminum and aluminum alloy spreads heat quickly and evenly throughout pan.

- **Layers 6 and 8:** Silver bonding agent/heat transfer.

- **Layer 7: Pure Aluminum** – Spreads heat quickly across the bottom of the pan

- **Layer 9: Surgical Stainless Steel** – Long lasting beauty, easy cleaning and induction compatible.

"Healthy cooking is more than food selection. It is also how you prepare foods" **American *Heart Association***

Patented Ultra-Temp™ Control & Whistle Valve

The only cookware in the world with a patented, precisely calibrated Temperature Gauge that extends down inside the pan through the cover knob to provide the cooking temperature inside the pan – just like an oven. This feature assures you of the correct cooking temperature without having to lift the cover, ensuring precious minerals, vitamins and life-giving enzymes are not lost during the cooking process

The patented, Ultra-Temp™ control and whistle valve tells you when to lower the heat, so you will never burn a meal again. Ultra-Tech II™ takes the guesswork out of cooking.

Easy-to-Remove Temperature Gauge

The easy-to-remove temperature gauge can be used to check the internal temperature of chicken, steaks and chops when pan-broiling without a cover, and when roasting on top of the stove.

Test for Doneness by inserting thermometer into center of meat.

Rare: red 140°F (60°C)   3 to 4 minutes per side

Medium-rare: dark pink 150°F (66°C)   4 to 5 minutes per side

Medium: light pink 160°F (71°C)   5 to 6 minutes per side

Well-done: dry 170°F (77°C) 6 to 7 minutes per side

The USDA recommends cooking whole cuts of meat to 145°F (63°C), measured with the temperature gauge inserted into the thickest part of the meat. Always allow cooked meat to rest three minutes before carving. This does not apply to ground beef, veal, lamb and pork, which should be cooked to 160°F (71°C), with no rest time required. A safe cooking temperature for poultry, including ground chicken and turkey, is 165°F (74°C). Fresh or raw ham should be cooked to 160°F (71°C). Pre-cooked ham should be reheated to 140°F (60°C).

Ultra-Seal™ Cover Design - Vapor Seal

Specially balanced and weighted covers are designed to form a vapor seal between the pan and the cover. Vapors condense on the inside of the cover and collect in the scientifically engineered "water well" around the rim of the pan, creating the Ultra-Seal™ vacuum. Cooks vegetables and fruits in their own natural juices without adding water, thereby preserving valuable vitamins, minerals, flavors and life-giving enzymes. It's the largest, scientifically engineered water well in the industry.

Ultra-Grip™ Stay Cool Handles

Ultra-Grip™ handles are ergonomically designed to provide a secure, comfortable, textured safety grip that will not slip. Made of durable phenolic, our handles stay cool on top of the range, are dishwasher safe and ovenproof to 375°F (190°C).

Extra Long Stainless Steel Flame Guards

The durable stainless steel attachment screw and flame guard will not corrode or loosen, keeping handles tight and secure. Extra-long flame guards protect your handles from getting hot.

Self-Storing Trivet Covers & Built-in Lid Holder

Makes it easy to store inverted inside the pan (with the temperature gauge removed to its storage container), saving cabinet space. Enjoy the convenience of the Ultra-Tech II™ built-in lid holder in the handle. Additionally, by removing the temperature gauge, covers can be inverted as a trivet with pans nesting neatly inside for the convenience of tableside service.

Combination & Stack Cooking

Your Ultra-Tech II Cooking System is designed to provide even heat distribution and the Ultra-Seal™ needed for combination and stack cooking. Cook an entire meal... roast, vegetables, gravy, cake and apples on top of the stove. This is especially convenient around the holidays when burner space is limited and it cooks in half the time of oven cooking.

For Combination Cooking, follow the directions for the Roast Beef Dinner. After adding the vegetables to the 6-quart roaster, place the 6-cup/steamer rack on the roaster to form a platform for baking the cake. Invert the 2-quart Junior Dome Cover and add your favorite cake mix. Cover with the large high dome lid to create a Dutch oven and form the Ultra-Seal™.

For example, to stack cook, fill the 2-quart covered saucepan with quartered apples and cook over medium heat with the Ultra-Temp™ control and whistle valve open. When the whistle sounds, close the valve and stack the 2-quart saucepan on top of the Dutch oven cover, and cook the entire meal on one burner. Combination stack cooking saves time, energy and food dollars!

Induction Cooking

An induction-cooking element (a "burner") is a powerful, high-frequency electromagnet, with the electromagnetism generated by sophisticated electronics in the "element" under the unit's ceramic surface. When an Ultra-Tech II™ pan is placed in the generating magnetic field, the field transfers ("induces") energy into the induction compatible outer layer of metal. The transferred energy causes the metal to become hot. By controlling the strength of the electromagnetic field, we can control the amount of heat being generated in the pan instantaneously. It's the Ultra-Tech II™ pan that generates the heat directly, not the induction cooker.

Induction Cooking Guidelines

No.	Setting	Function	Temperature	Guidelines
1		Warm	100°F (38°C)	110°F (43°C) Rendering chocolate, yogurt
2	Low	Warm	150°F (66°C)	Pasteurizing, slow cooking
3	Med-Low	Simmer	180°F (82°C)	Simmering stocks, melting cheese, sauces
4		Simmer	210°F (99°C)	Waterless cooking, jellies, jams, baking
5	Medium	Boiling	240°F (116°C)	Sauté, boil, steaming, roasting, eggs, crepes
6		Boiling	300°F (150°C)	Sauté vegetables, pancakes, French toast
7		Browning	330°F (166°C)	Stir fry, sauté meat, grill sandwiches
8	Med-High	Frying	360°F (182°C)	Deep fry in oil; fritters, chicken, donuts, fries
9		Pan Broil	390°F (199°C)	Popcorn, Pan Broil chops, steaks, and chickens
10	High	Sear	450°F (232°C)	Searing meats before roasting

7

Recipe Features

Each recipe found in this cookbook provides quick, at-a-glance nutritional recipe information, in the same place on every recipe page. This feature allows you to quickly see all the information you need. For instance, preparation time is the second feature for every recipe. If you have surprise guests for dinner, or an unexpected interruption, this feature lets you know quickly if you have enough time to prepare the recipe.

Number of Servings: If the recipe is designed for eight servings and you know you need only four, divide all the ingredients in half before preparing.

Preparation Time: So you can plan when to begin preparation and the approximate time the meal will be served.

Equipment: The proper cooking utensil is called for in every recipe. Never again will you be pouring from one pan into another because there is not enough room in the first utensil.

NOTE: On the side of every Ultra-Tech II™ pan, under the logo, you will find the pan description or quart size of that particular pan.

Ingredients: Everything you need is in one column – no searching necessary. See table for metric conversions.

Preparation: Short, to-the-point descriptions of each step.

Example of Nutritional Breakdown:

NUTRITIONAL BREAKDOWN PER SERVING: Calories; Fat Grams; Carbohydrate Grams; Protein Grams; Cholesterol mg; Sodium mg.

METRIC CONVERSION CHART

Comparison to Metric Measure

Description	Symbol	Multiply By	To Find	Symbol
Teaspoons	tsp.	5.0	milliliters	ml
Tablespoons	tbsp.	15.0	milliliters	ml
Fluid ounces	fl. Oz.	30.0	milliliters	ml
Cups	c	0.24	liters	l
Pints	pt.	.47	liters	l
Quarts	qt.	.95	liters	l
Ounces	o.	28.0	grams	g
Pounds	lb.	0.45	kilograms	kg
Fahrenheit	F	5/9 (after subtracting 32)		
Celsius	C			

Liquid Measure to Milliliters

¼ teaspoon	=	1.25 milliliters
½ teaspoon	=	2.50 milliliters
¾ teaspoon	=	3.75 milliliters
1 teaspoon	=	5.00 milliliters
1¼ teaspoons	=	6.25 milliliters
1½ teaspoons	=	7.50 milliliters
1¾ teaspoons	=	8.75 milliliters
2 teaspoons	=	10.0 milliliters
1 tablespoon	=	15.0 milliliters
2 tablespoons	=	30.0 milliliters

Liquid Measure to Liters

¼ cup	=	0.06 liters
½ cup	=	0.12 liters
¾ cup	=	0.18 liters
1 cup	=	0.24 liters
1¼ cups	=	0.30 liters
1½ cups	=	0.36 liters
2 cups	=	0.48 liters
2½ cups	=	0.60 liters
3 cups	=	0.72 liters
3½ cups	=	0.84 liters
4 cups	=	0.96 liters
4½ cups	=	1.08 liters
5 cups	=	1.20 liters
5½ cups	=	1.32 liters

CHAPTER 2

Ultra-Tech II™ - Use & Care

Congratulations on your decision to invest in the Ultra Tech II™ Nutritional Cooking System from Carico. Your decision will pay lifelong dividends in healthful, flavorful and nutritional meals. The Ultra-Temp™ temperature control and whistle valve assures you of maximum food value retention and allows you to prepare your foods without water or added fats. Take a moment to acquaint yourself with the proper use and care of this fine cookware. By following a few simple steps, you will enjoy the maximum benefits of, and become an expert in, the art of Waterless, Greaseless Cooking.

The Ultra-Seal™ Method

Mother Nature designed foods to give us everything we need, naturally. Fresh foods contain abundant flavors, vitamins, minerals, digestive enzymes and color. However, most cooking methods can rob fresh food of its natural qualities. Fortunately, the Ultra-Seal™ method of Ultra-Tech II™ cookware saves money, work, time, energy, flavor, vitamins, minerals and life-giving enzymes. Waterless cooking is possible because a vapor seal is created between the cover and the rim of the pan (water-well). Heat is distributed across the extra-heavy bottom of the 18/10 304 surgical stainless steel Ultra-Core™ base, up the pan sides and through the cover.

This process cooks food in its own natural moisture for nutritious, flavor-filled meals. Food shrinkage is greatly reduced, making waterless, greaseless cooking more economical than ordinary cooking methods. The Ultra-Seal™ is maintained by using low heat with the cover on and the whistle valve closed. Therefore, Ultra-Tech II™ cookware is the most energy efficient cookware on the market. The Ultra-Seal™ method retains the nutritional value of your food by eliminating the following processes that rob fresh food of its natural goodness.

1. **No Need to Peel** fruits and vegetables. Peeling removes the vitamins and minerals directly beneath the skin. With Ultra-Tech II™ cookware, a good scrubbing is all that is necessary for cooking the waterless way.

2. **No Water Needed.** Minerals and vitamins in fruits and vegetables are water soluble. For example, when carrots are cooked in water, the water turns orange and is then poured down the drain along with the minerals, vitamins and flavor. Salt and butter is then added to replace lost flavor. With the Ultra-Seal™ method, vegetables are cooked waterless, in a vapor seal, at controlled temperatures. Vegetables and fruits come to the table garden fresh, rich in flavor and color, without the need for the high calories and health risks of butter, oil and salt.

3. **No Need to Boil.** Boiling and microwaving sterilizes fruits and vegetables, killing life-giving enzymes. For example, when milk is pasteurized, it's heated to approximately 160°F (71°C) to kill bacteria, then quickly cooled. If the milk was heated above 160°F (71°C) the life-giving enzymes would be destroyed and the milk would begin to spoil

within a matter of hours. With the Ultra-Seal™ method, vegetables are cooked, at controlled temperatures, in their own natural juices, in a waterless vapor seal. Vegetables and fruits come to the table garden fresh, rich in minerals, vitamins and life-giving enzymes.

4. **No Oxidation.** Oxidation of food occurs when cooking without a cover, thereby exposing food to air while reducing the quality of the food significantly. For example, when you cut an apple in half and allow it to sit uncovered, it begins to oxidize and turn brown. When vegetables are cooked the waterless way in Ultra-Tech II™ cookware, with the cover on, forming the Ultra-Seal™, they are cooked in a partial vacuum, thereby preventing oxidation and keeping the aroma and natural goodness in the pan. For example, you will not know if broccoli or cabbage is being cooked until the cover is removed.

5. **No Need for High Heat.** High heat cooking causes food to dehydrate and shrink. For example, when you smell a roast cooking in the oven, you're really smelling the natural meat juices that have been transformed into vapor. The high temperature combined with open cooking greatly adds to meat shrinkage. Meat roasted or pan broiled, on top of stove, using the Ultra-Seal™ method of medium-to-low heat, retains the natural juices and flavors, decreasing meat shrinkage dramatically. You save money!

6. **No Need for Fat, Butter or Oil.** Sautéing and frying in fat, butter or oil adds excessive calories, making food seven times harder to digest. Using the Ultra-Seal™ method, the natural properties of the food keeps it from sticking to the high quality 18/10 304 surgical stainless steel pan. Plus, the Ultra-Seal™ method retains natural flavors; there is no need to add salt, butter or oil during or after cooking to replace lost flavor.

NOTE: The Ultra-Seal™ retains the moisture in foods with a water seal around the inset cover of the pan. Sometimes, when a pan is allowed to cool, the condensed moisture inside the pan creates a vacuum causing the lid to lock onto the pan. Should this happen with Ultra-Tech II™, simply open the whistle vent, thereby releasing the vacuum seal, enabling the cover to remove easily.

Cleaning Before First Use

Before using your Ultra Tech II™ cookware for the first time, wash each piece thoroughly in a basin of warm soapy water with 1 cup of white distilled vinegar added. This initial soaking is essential to ensure that all the polishing compounds are removed before cooking food. After this initial washing, normal washing is all that is necessary to clean your cookware. Occasional cleaning with a stainless steel cleaner like Barkeeper's Friend or Kleen King is recommended.

NOTICE: Before washing, remove the Ultra-Temp™ temperature gauge and place it in its storage container. Do not put the temperature gauge in the dishwasher.

Cleaning the Patented Ultra-Temp™ Control Valve

Periodic washing of the Ultra-Temp™ control valve is recommended. To do so, simply remove the thermometer and unscrew the knob assembly. Wash the parts in hot soapy water. Rinse and dry thoroughly before reassembling. Additionally, always wash the thermometer after testing internal food temperatures.

Regular Cleaning of Ultra-Tech II Cookware

After each use, wash cookware in warm soapy water using a dish cloth or nylon plastic net. DO NOT use metal scouring pads, as they may scratch the high polished outside surface. (If using a metal scouring pad, use it on the inside and the bottom of the pan only.) Rinse and dry. Dishwasher safe but handwashing is recommended.

Surface Care

You can use Carico stainless steel utensils in the cookware. However, never cut food in the cookware, as this could mar the surface.

Cleaning Stubborn Spots

Occasionally, when cooking starchy foods or searing meats, a stain may appear on the inside surface of the pan. A blue or golden brown discoloration may also appear on the pan from overheating the unit. These stains are easily removed with a good, non-abrasive stainless steel cleaner, such as Bar Keepers Friend or Kleen King. First, make a paste with the cleaner and a small amount of water. Using a paper towel or soft cloth, rub the paste over the stained area, rinse and dry.

During the first few times of use, bright metal marks may appear on the inside of your pans. Remove these and other minor scratches by placing a small amount of stainless steel cleaner into a dry pan, and polish in a circular motion with a damp paper towel or dishcloth. Then, rinse in warm soapy water, rinse and dry.

While surgical stainless steel is an extremely durable metal, it is not impervious to corrosion, pitting or spotting. Foods such as mustard, mayonnaise, lemon juice, tomatoes, tomato paste, vinegar, salt, dressings or condiments may etch stainless steel if allowed to remain in contact with the surface for a long period of time. Strong bleaches can have the same effect.

Pitting may result if undissolved salt is allowed to remain on the bottom of the pan. Pitting looks like small white spots, and does not in any way affect the performance or usefulness of your pans, nor are they a defect in the metal or the workmanship. To avoid pitting, salt should only be added to boiling liquid and stirred until it is completely dissolved.

Burned Foods

If the cookware is used properly, foods should not burn; however, in the event they do burn, fill the hot pan with warm water and let soak while you enjoy your meal. If burned on foods are not easily removed by normal washing, partially fill the pan with water and bring to a boil to loosen the food, then clean with stainless steel cleaner, rinse and dry.

CHAPTER 3

Waterless Cooking

It's reassuring to know that all fresh vegetables have a natural, built-in supply of vital vitamins, minerals and digestive enzymes. For better health, it's important to retain these nutrients when cooking. Healthy cooking with Ultra-Tech II™ waterless, greaseless cookware will greatly aid you in **Cooking for a Longer, Healthier Life.**

No Need to Peel

With Ultra-Tech II™ waterless, greaseless cooking, delicious vegetables can be prepared without sacrificing the wonders of nature. The first major breakthrough of this unique cooking method eliminates the need to strip away the flavor in the nutrient-rich skin. For most vegetables, a gentle scrubbing is all that's needed before cooking. One more step to ensure that all of nature's goodness arrives "garden fresh" at your table.

Use the Correct Size Saucepan

Vegetables should nearly fill the saucepan. Add Carico purified water to cover vegetables and allow the vegetables to soak for a few minutes, then drain. This restores the natural moisture lost between and during harvesting and transit.

Medium to Low is All You Need to Know

Cover the pan, open the Ultra-Temp™ control and whistle valve, then place the pan over medium heat. When the whistle sounds the temperature gauge should register between 160-195°F (71-91°C) (in the center of the cooking range of the thermometer). Close the whistle valve and reduce the heat to low to create a vapor seal (Ultra-Seal™). When the cover spins freely on a cushion of water, the vapor seal is formed. Begin timing the vegetables. As a general rule, allow 8 to 10 minutes per quart-size pan for crisp, tender, fresh vegetables, and 12 to 15 minutes per quart for more tender or soft-cooked root vegetables (carrots, potatoes, beets, turnips, etc.).

Don't Peek

During the waterless cooking process, don't peek. Removing the cover will compromise the vapor seal, lengthen the cooking time and may cause the vegetables to burn. If you or another member of the family does lift the lid, lower the heat, cover the pan, close the vent and add 2 tablespoons of water to the rim to reestablish the vapor seal. When the lid spins freely on a cushion of moisture, the vapor seal has formed. Add 3 to 5 minutes to the prescribed cooking time.

Ultra-Temp™ Control and Whistle Valve

The patented Ultra-Temp™ control and whistle valve is one of the most unique features of the Ultra-Tech II™ cooking system. The precisely calibrated, patented temperature gauge and control valve eliminates the need for guesswork, making it easy to achieve perfect cooking results.

If the heat is too low, below 160°F (71°C), the Ultra-Seal™ will not form and the vegetables will not cook. If the heat is too high, above 195°F (91°C) and the whistle valve is closed for waterless cooking, the cover will spit moisture and the vegetables could burn. The perfect cooking temperature for cooking vegetables the waterless way is between 160-195°F (71-91°C) as indicated on the Ultra-Temp™ temperature gauge.

With Ultra-Tech II™ "flavor-sealing" covered cookware, vegetables can be cooked using low heat, eliminating the need for boiling in water and sautéing in oil. With low heat, the vegetables are cooked in a "waterless" environment, quickly and evenly in a vacuum seal below the boiling temperature, or "greaseless" without oil, and prepared in their own natural moisture. Using the vegetable's natural juices eliminates the need to add water or oil during cooking.

Adapting Recipes

This cookbook is written by culinary professionals and experienced cooks using Ultra-Tech II™ waterless, greaseless cookware. To enjoy the benefits of cooking without water and added fats, you will need to learn to adapt recipes. The easiest way to do this is to trust your Ultra-Tech II™ cookware while following the instructions and recipes in this book.

Jersey Sweet Corn-on-the-Cob

Serves: 4 to 6
Preparation Time: 25 minutes
Equipment: chef knife, 11-inch covered fry/sauté pan

4-6   ears of corn in the husk

To prepare 4 to 6 ears of corn, remove the husks and silks. Place enough clean husks in the pan to completely cover the bottom. This will prevent the corn starch and natural sugars from scorching on the bottom of the pan. Rinse with Carico purified water and drain.

Note: You may want to cut the ears of corn in half, quarters or one inch wheels.

Place the corn on the husks. Rinse again with Carico purified water and pour most of the water off. The water that clings to the corn and husks is sufficient to cook the waterless way. Cover the pan with the Ultra-Temp™ control with the whistle valve open and place the pan over medium heat. When the whistle sounds, the temperature gauge should register between 160-195°F (71-91°C), in the center of the cooking range of the thermometer. Close the whistle valve and reduce the heat to low to create a vapor seal (Ultra-Seal™). Spin the cover. When the cover spins freely on a cushion of moisture the vapor seal is formed. Begin timing the vegetables. Corn-on-the-cob will cook in 25 to 30 minutes in the 11-inch fry/sauté pan.

Test the corn-on-the-cob for doneness. If not done, cover the pan, close the Ultra-Temp™ control and whistle valve and add 2 tablespoons of Carico purified water to the rim to reestablish the Ultra-Seal™. Spin the cover. The vapor seal is formed when the cover spins freely on a cushion of moisture. Cook over low heat for 5 to 7 minutes.

Potatoes, Sweet Potatoes, Yams and Root Vegetables

The first major breakthrough of this unique cooking method eliminates the need to strip away the flavor in nutrient-rich skin. For most root vegetables, a gentle scrubbing is all that's needed before cooking. One more step to ensure that all of nature's goodness arrives "garden fresh" at your table.

Potatoes, parsnips, sweet potatoes, yams, beets and other root vegetables can be cut into halves or quarters to shorten cooking time. Fill the pan with the root vegetable, skin side against the utensil, rinse with Carico purified water and pour off most of the water. The small amount of water left in the pan and the moisture that clings to the vegetable is sufficient for cooking root vegetables the waterless way.

Cover the pan with the Ultra-Temp™ control with the whistle valve open and place the pan over medium heat. When the whistle sounds, the Ultra-Temp™ temperature gauge should register between 160-195°F (71-91°), which is in the center of the cooking range of the thermometer. Close the whistle valve and reduce the heat to low to create a vapor seal (Ultra-Seal™). When the cover spins freely on a cushion of moisture, the vapor seal is formed. Begin timing the vegetables.

Cook Frozen Vegetables the Waterless Way

Do not defrost. Place the frozen vegetables in the pan they most nearly fill. Rinse with Carico purified water and pour water off. The water that clings to the vegetables and its own natural moisture are sufficient for cooking the waterless way.

Cover the pan, open the whistle valve and cook over medium heat. When the whistle sounds, the Ultra-Temp™ temperature gauge should register between 160-195°F (71-91°C) which is in the center of the cooking range of the thermometer. Close the whistle valve and reduce the heat to low to create a vapor seal (Ultra-Seal™). When the lid spins freely on a cushion of moisture, the vapor seal is formed. Begin timing the vegetables.

Some Recipes Need Water

Some recipes require adding water or liquid to cook with, such as dried beans, rice, pasta, soup, stews and sauces. Remember, waterless for vegetables and greaseless for meat, poultry, and some seafood.

Some Foods & Recipes Need Oil

Some fish and foods with a flour, breadcrumb and/or egg base have no natural lubricant and will require adding a small amount of oil or unsalted butter to the pan to prevent sticking. See Pan Frying and Eggs for more details.

The Art of Stir-Frying Vegetables

In China, where fuel supplies are limited, cooking foods quickly has always been a priority. Vegetables and other ingredients are carefully cut into bite size pieces or thin sliced to cook in only 3 to 5 minutes.

How it Works: Cover the 11-inch fry/sauté pan with the Ultra-Temp™ control with whistle valve open and place the pan over medium-high heat. When the Ultra-Temp™ temperature gauge registers in the RED about 200°F (93°C), uncover the pan and add 1 to 2 tablespoons of oil.

Add vegetables and cook, tossing quickly and constantly until they are crisp and tender, about 3 to 4 minutes. Quick cooking will seal in the fresh flavors, juices and valuable nutrients.

When stir-frying a mixture of vegetables, place longer-cooking vegetables in the skillet and partially cook before adding the more tender vegetables. For slightly softer vegetables, cover the pan and reduce to low heat for the final minutes of cooking.

Cooking for One or Two

When cooking for one or two people, the quantity of vegetables used will naturally be reduced. However, with Ultra-Tech II™ waterless cooking, more than one vegetable can be cooked in the same pan, at the same time, the waterless way. Potatoes, sliced carrots and broccoli can be cooked together with no interchanging of flavors or colors.

For example, using a 1-quart saucepan or 1.7-quart saucepan/skillet, place the potatoes in the pan, halved or whole, with the skin side to the surface of the pan. Add two carrots (sliced) and top with frozen corn and broccoli florets. Rinse the vegetables with Carico purified water and pour off most of the water. Cook as directed.

CHAPTER 4

Greaseless Cooking

Because of the easy-to-clean, high-quality, non-porous 304 surgical stainless steel cooking surface of Ultra-Tech II™ cookware, meats can be seared without using high-calorie oils and fats. This process of searing and browning, known as "caramelization," brings the natural salts and sugars to the surface of the meat to form an intensely flavored crust, while locking in the natural juices.

Ultra-Tech II™ allows you to pan broil chicken, steak, chops; roast beef, veal and pork, or bake a meatloaf on top of the range without adding grease, fat or butter. Entrées come to the table deliciously juicy and tender, eliminating costly meat shrinkage often seen with oven cooking.

Seven Ways to Cook Meat

There are SEVEN techniques for cooking meats the greaseless way: Pan broiling, roasting, braising, sautéing, baking, pan frying and steaming.

Throughout this section, you will learn the methods of cooking a roast on top of the stove, preparing the perfect steak, baking a meatloaf, along with the quick and easy methods associated with braising, sautéing, pan frying and steaming. All of the recipes are cooked on top of the stove.

Pan Broiling

Because heat is conducted to the meat very efficiently through Ultra-Tech II™ cookware, the meat's surface tends to brown evenly and very quickly, in 1 to 2 minutes. Once the meat is browned sufficiently, it will release easily from the pan for turning. To prevent the surface of the meat from toughening while the inside cooks, the heat is usually reduced after the initial browning or searing. If the pan is covered with the Ultra-Temp™ control with the whistle vent closed, vapor is trapped and a process similar to basting results. Therefore, you must open the whistle vent when pan-broiling or leave the lid ajar. When sautéing or pan frying, you may want to leave the pan uncovered.

Deglaze for Creating a Pan Sauce

After removing meats, stir in 1 cup (0.24 liters) of liquid (chicken stock, beef stock, veal stock or wine) and stir to loosen juices from the pan. For a thicker sauce, reduce over medium heat until desired thickness is achieved.

Pan Broiling Example:

Lemon Sesame Chicken

Serves: 4

Time: 20 minutes

Equipment: 8 or 10-inch chef knife, cutting board, 11-inch covered
fry/sauté skillet or electric skillet

4	skinless chicken breasts
1	fresh lemon, juice thereof
1	tablespoon toasted sesame seeds
1	teaspoon freshly chopped oregano

Preheat the covered skillet for 4 to 5 minutes over medium heat. When the Ultra-Temp™ temperature gauge registers between 160-195°F (71-91°C) the surface of the skillet is hot enough to sear the meat and lock in the natural juices. Remove the cover and add the chicken to the pan, pressing it against the bottom. The chicken will stick at first; cook uncovered until the chicken is browned and releases easily from the pan, 7 to 8 minutes. Turn and sear on the other side, 5 to 7 minutes.

Test for doneness by inserting the temperature gauge into the center of the chicken. The USDA recommended safe internal temperature for chicken is a minimum of 165°F (73°C).

NOTE: When you take the chicken out of the pan, do not cut into it right away. Doing so will allow the liquid to pool out and your perfectly pan-broiled, moist chicken breast will end up dry. By letting it rest for 3 or 4 minutes, the moisture is redistributed and your chicken will be tender and juicy.

To serve, sprinkle with fresh lemon juice and top with sesame seeds and oregano.

Alternative Method

Cut a fresh lemon in half and squeeze the juice into the hot skillet to deglaze the pan. Place the halved lemon in the skillet, cut side down, and with a fork move the lemon across the surface to loosen chicken drippings. Spoon juice over chicken, sprinkle with sesame seeds and oregano.

How to Cook Perfect Steaks & Chops

When searing steaks and chops, pan broil with the cover ajar and the Ultra-Temp™ control and whistle valve open, thereby allowing the steaks or chops to cook quicker and be juicer. Crowding the pan, or cooking at too low a temperature and covering, may cause the meat to steam. Practice makes perfect, and a good home chef learns to cook steaks and chops to the desired doneness using high-quality Ultra-Tech II™ skillets, proper cooking techniques, and by checking the internal temperature of the meat with the Ultra-Temp™ temperature gauge. Because of different textures, cuts and thickness of meat, learning to cook a delicious steak, using the Ultra-Temp™ temperature gauge, will provide you with perfect results every time.

Steaks & Chops	Approximate Cooking Time
Rare: red center 140°F (60°C)	3 to 4 minutes per side
Medium-rare: dark red 150°F (66°C)	4 to 5 minutes per side
Medium: light pink 160°F (71°C)	6 to 7 minutes per side
Well-done: dry 170°F (77°C)	7 to 8 minutes per side

Test for doneness by inserting the Ultra-Temp™ temperature gauge into the center of the meat. The USDA recommended safe internal temperature for pork is a minimum of 155°F (68°C).

Roasting on top of the Stove

Roasts and whole poultry that might otherwise be cooked in an oven can now be roasted on top of the range in Ultra-Tech II™ cookware in a relatively short period of time. The extra-heavy bottom of Ultra-Tech II™ 9-ply Ultra-Core™ allows you to sear and brown meats first and then roast on top of the stove, at medium temperatures, for a given doneness.

Instructions for roasting on top of the stove are relatively simple to follow. Always roast meat in the smallest size utensil into which it will fit.

This will result in a tender, juicy cut, and will reduce meat shrinkage. Roasting time is reduced by about half for unstuffed, skinned poultry, as well as beef, pork, veal and lamb.

Begin with meat that is nearly room temperature. To roast, preheat the appropriate size utensil over medium heat with the cover on and the whistle valve closed, about 3 to 4 minutes. When the Ultra-Temp™ temperature gauge reads between 160-195°F (71-91°C), the pan is hot enough to begin the searing process. Remove the cover and place roast in the pan, pressing against the bottom to brown evenly. Meat will stick at first but will loosen when seared properly, about 5 to 7 minutes per side. Sear meat on all sides.

Cover the pan and open the Ultra-Temp™ control and whistle valve. When the whistle sounds, close the whistle valve and reduce the heat to low. Roast to desired doneness according to the chart below. Proper roasting temperature can be determined by tiny bubbles forming around the base of the cover. If water bubbles spit, the heat is too high. Reduce the temperature so only tiny bubbles appear around the rim. Cooking time begins after searing (browning) the meat on all sides, covering and forming the Ultra-Seal™.

Desired Doneness	Approximate Minutes per Pound
Rare: red center 140°F (60°C)	9-10 minutes - beef
Medium-rare: dark red center 150°F (66°C)	11-12 minutes - beef
Medium: light pink center 160°F (71°C)	14-15 minutes - pork
Medium-well: moist 165°F (74°C)	17-18 minutes - poultry
Well-done: dry 170°F (77°C)	19-20 minutes

Test for doneness by inserting the Ultra-Temp™ temperature gauge into the center of the meat. The USDA recommended safe internal temperature for pork is a minimum of 155°F (68°C), and poultry 165°F (74°C).

Roast Beef Dinner

Serves: 8

Time: depends on desired doneness. See previous page.

Equipment: 8 or 10-inch chef knife, 6-quart (5.7 L) roaster/saucepan, Ultra-Temp™ cover or large dome cover

4-5	pound eye round or sirloin tip roast
½	cup white wine
2	stalks celery, minced or grated
1	medium onion, minced
2	medium carrots, grated
8	medium red potatoes
8	medium carrots, quartered
2	medium onion, quartered

Begin with meat that is nearly room temperature. To roast, preheat the 6-quart (5.7 L) roaster/saucepan over medium heat with the cover on and the whistle valve closed, about 3 to 4 minutes. When the Ultra-Temp™ temperature gauge reads between 160-195°F (71-91°C), the pan is hot enough to begin the searing process. Remove the cover and place the meat in the pan, pressing against the bottom to brown evenly. Meat will stick at first but will loosen when seared properly, about 5 to 7 minutes per side. Sear meat on all sides.

After searing, add the wine to deglaze the pan and reduce the heat to low. Add the celery, minced onions and grated carrots, then arrange the larger cut vegetables around the roast to cook. To obtain the proper cooking temperature for roasting, the cover must spin freely on a cushion of moisture, emitting tiny bubbles. If water bubbles spit the heat is too high. Reduce the temperature so only tiny bubbles appear around the rim. Cooking time begins after forming the Ultra-Seal™. Roast to desired doneness according to the time chart.

Combination Stack Cooking

Your Ultra-Tech II™ Cooking System and the Ultra-Seal™ is designed to provide the even heat distribution needed for combination cooking.

Combination Cooking is a wonderful convenience. You can prepare a Roast Beef Dinner for 6 to 8 people using the 6-quart roaster/saucepan, 6-cup/steamer rack as a platform and an inverted 2-quart Junior Dome Cover to bake a cake, and covered with the Large Dome Cover to create a Dutch oven.

To stack cook, fill the 2-quart covered saucepan with quartered apples and cook over medium heat with the Ultra-Temp™ control and whistle valve open. When the whistle sounds, close the whistle vent and stack the 2-quart sauce pan on top of the Large Dome Dutch oven Cover. Combination cooking is especially convenient around the holidays when burner space is limited and the entire meal cooks on a single burner in half the time of oven cooking. Combination stack cooking saves time, energy and food dollars!

Sautéing

The official definition of sautéing is "a food that is fried in a small amount of fat," over medium heat, stirring occasionally to prevent sticking or burning.

Because of the Ultra-Tech II™ easy-to-clean, non-porous 304 surgical stainless steel cooking surface, and the superior Ultra-Core's™ heat conduction, meats and vegetables can be sautéed without using high-calorie oils and fats. This process is a combination of searing and browning, called "caramelization," which brings the natural salts and sugars to the surface of the meats and vegetables to form an intensely flavored crust, thereby locking in natural juices and producing a more professional and classic end result.

Braising – Cooking in Liquids

Cooking in liquids, or "braising," is particularly good for a variety of entrees, and perfect for tougher, less expensive cuts of meat and poultry.

Cover the skillet or 6-quart roaster/saucepan with the Ultra-Temp™ cover, close the control and whistle vent and place over medium heat. When the Ultra-Temp™ temperature gauge reads between 160-195°F (71-91°C), about 3 to 4 minutes, uncover, add the meat or poultry and cook until seared and browned on all sides. Add ¼ to ½ cup of broth, stock, wine or Carico purified water, as indicated in the recipe. Cover with the whistle valve open. When the whistle sounds, close the control valve, spin the cover to form the Ultra-Seal™ and reduce the heat to low. The inside temperature will drop to the low end of the central cooking range, about 160°F (70°C). Simmer according to time chart.

Meat type	Cooking Time (Minutes per pound)
Beef & Lamb	20-25
Pork & Veal	25-30
Venison	20-25
All Poultry	15-20
Duck & Goose	25-30

Pan Frying Seafood or Floured and Breaded Meats

Pan frying with a small amount of oil or unsalted butter is recommended for floured and breaded meats, as well as most seafood. With the exception of tuna, salmon and swordfish, (which can be pan broiled the greaseless way in a similar method to steaks, chops and chicken), most seafood contains very little natural oils. Add a little oil or unsalted butter to the pan prior to adding seafood, or meats that have been floured or breaded. Pan fry over medium to medium-high heat. Cook about 3 to 5 minutes per side and test for desired doneness.

Steaming Meats, Shellfish and Seafood

Steaming Units:

The 6-cup Steamer Rack fits the 6-quart Roaster/Saucepan and the 11-inch Fry/Sauté Skillet. The 2-quart Steamer Inset fits the 2 and 3-quart saucepans.

There are a few exceptions to cooking meats the waterless and greaseless way. Some recipes call for braising or steaming meats. Steaming can be an excellent method to remove excess fat from ground beef, lamb or venison.

To Steam Meats: Place the **Steamer Inset** (fits 2 and 3 quart saucepans) into the pan, add 2-3 cups of Carico purified water, stock, wine or beer, and bring to a boil over medium heat. Add meat to steamer inset and cover with the whistle valve open or lid ajar. Steam about 15 minutes per pound. Live lobster, crabs, mussels and clams are best steamed in wine or beer. When the alcohol is released during the boiling process, the seafood is gently put to sleep, relaxing the muscles and tenderizing the meat, resulting in food cooked to perfection.

Top-of-the-Range Baking

Ultra-Tech II™ cookware is designed to bake cakes, cornbread, cookies, casseroles, meatloaf, ribs and lasagna, on top of the range, more efficiently than in the oven. For example, to bake a small cake, preheat a 1.7-quart or 3-quart saucepan over medium heat. Coat the pan with a small amount of unsalted butter (or coat with non-stick cooking spray). Pour the cake batter into the pan until the pan is half full, cover and open the Ultra-Temp™ control and whistle valve. When the whistle sounds, reduce the heat to low and finish baking (about 12-15 minutes). The temperature gauge should register between 160-195°F (71-91°C), in the center of the cooking range of the thermometer. Higher altitudes may require longer baking times.

Note: Foods with crust toppings, as well as pies and some breads, will not brown.

Top of the Range Baking, Example:

Carico Meatloaf

On top of the stove
Serves: 8
Preparation Time: 1 hour
Equipment: 8 or 10-inch chef knife, cutting board, large stainless mixing
bowl and 11-inch covered fry/sauté skillet

1½	pounds lean ground beef, veal, pork, chicken, turkey, or a combination
½	medium onion, chopped
½	green pepper, seeded and chopped
1	stalk celery, chopped
1	cup Italian breadcrumbs or oatmeal
½	teaspoon dried or fresh chopped oregano
1	teaspoon dried or fresh chopped basil
1	egg or 2 egg whites
1	cup sharp cheese, shredded (optional)
1	cup ketchup or tomato sauce

In a large mixing bowl, combine all the ingredients and mix well. Press meatloaf mix into large skillet. Cover, open the Ultra-Temp™ control and whistle valve, and place over medium heat. When the whistle sounds, 3-5 minutes, close the whistle valve, reduce the heat to low and bake 35-45 minutes. The temperature gauge should register between 160-195°F (71-91°C), in the center of the cooking range of the thermometer. Begin timing the meatloaf.

To obtain the proper cooking temperature for baking on top of the stove, the cover must spin freely on a cushion of moisture emitting tiny bubbles. If the cover spits moisture, the temperature is too hot; lower the heat slightly.

Variation: Top meatloaf mix with shredded sharp cheese, ketchup or tomato sauce. Cook as directed above.

To serve, slice meatloaf into 8 equal portions and plate. Serve with vegetables cooked the waterless way.

CHAPTER 5

Eggs, Omelets, Crepes & Pancakes

Eggs and egg-based foods are the exception to the greaseless cooking method. Having no natural oils, a small amount of lubricant, such as unsalted butter or oil, is required to prevent eggs and egg-based recipes from sticking to the pan.

USDA recommends: No one should eat foods containing raw eggs. This includes "health food" milk shakes made with raw eggs, Caesar salad, Hollandaise sauce, and any other foods like homemade mayonnaise, ice cream, or eggnog made from recipes in which the egg ingredients are not thoroughly cooked.

Preparation

Let's face it, eggs stick to every pan, even the inexpensive coated pans. However, when your Ultra-Tech II™ skillet is prepped correctly, it's the best non-stick stainless steel cookware on the market today.

Cleaning: Before cooking eggs, a quick scrub of the pan with Bar Keepers Friend or Kleen King stainless steel cleaner should be all that is needed to keep eggs from sticking to the pan.

Correct Size Pan: Although you can use any Ultra-Tech II™ pan to cook eggs and egg-based foods, using a pan that is too big, or having the heat too high, could cause the food to stick or burn. Food should nearly fill the pan; the Ultra-Tech II™ 9-inch gourmet skillet and 1.7-quart sauté/saucepan are best suited for cooking eggs and crepes. For large quantities of scrambled eggs or pancakes, we recommend the 11-inch gourmet skillet or 11-inch fry/sauté skillet; for even larger quantities use the 13-inch gourmet skillet.

Temperature: Medium to low is all you need to know. Preheat the pan over medium-low to medium heat, and melt unsalted butter or add oil. Add the eggs and reduce the heat to low. For induction 210-240°F (99-116°C). Pancakes and crepes cook best on medium heat, induction 240-270°F (99-116°C).

While experimenting, we suggest the use of unsalted butter as a lubricant to achieve the proper cooking temperature for eggs. Simply put, if the butter burns, the pan is too hot.

Fried Eggs

Preheat the 9-inch gourmet skillet over medium-low to medium heat, for induction 210-240°F (99-116°C). Place a small amount of unsalted butter in the pan, enough to cover the bottom when melted. When water bubbles release from the butter (2 to 3 minutes) and begin to pop, add eggs and reduce the heat slightly. When whites cook to desired firmness, flip eggs to cook on other side.

French Scrambled Eggs

Prepare eggs to scramble by placing eggs in bowl. Add 1 teaspoon of Carico purified water per egg and whip lightly with a whisk or fork.

Preheat the skillet over medium-low to medium heat, for induction 210-240°F (99-116°C). Place a small amount of unsalted butter in the pan, enough to cover the bottom when melted. When water bubbles release from butter (2 to 3 minutes) and begin to pop, add eggs. As eggs begin to cook, draw cooked part from the edge of the pan toward the center with a spatula, allowing uncooked eggs to move to hot surface of pan. Repeat process until eggs are scrambled to desired firmness.

Ham & Cheese Omelet

Prepare eggs for omelet by placing eggs in bowl. Add 1 teaspoon of Carico purified water per egg and whip lightly with a whisk or fork.

Preheat the skillet over medium-low to medium heat, for induction 210-240°F (99-116°C). Place a small amount of unsalted butter in pan, enough to cover the bottom when melted. When water bubbles release from butter (2 to 3 minutes) and begin to pop, add eggs and reduce the heat slightly.

The eggs will begin to cook and form to the pan. As it firms, shake to loosen. When eggs are nearly cooked, add grated cheese and ham, or other desired ingredients, to one half of the omelet. When cooked to desired firmness, loosen omelet and fold onto serving plate.

Soft and Hard Cooked Eggs, Example:

Soft Boiled & Hard Boiled Eggs

Serves: 4 – 6 eggs
Preparation Time: 15 minutes
Equipment: 1.7-quart (1.6 L) covered saucepan/sauté skillet

The perfect soft-cooked egg should have a warm runny yolk and a firm egg white. Preparing soft-cooked eggs can be tricky, but when you learn to cook with Ultra-Tech II™ cookware, soft-cooked eggs can be mastered on the first try.

Select a pan that the eggs to be cooked will completely cover the bottom of the pan. Place a folded paper towel in the bottom of the pan, and add 1 tablespoon Carico purified water per egg to wet the towel completely. Moisture in the paper towel will help to form the Ultra-Seal™.

Cover, open the Ultra-Temp™ whistle valve and adjust the temperature to medium heat. When the whistle sounds, close the whistle valve and reduce the heat to the lowest setting.

Set your timer for 8 minutes. Cook 7 minutes for a yolk that is still runny and 8 minutes for a yolk that is almost set. When the timer sounds, fill the pan with cold Carico purified water to stop the eggs from cooking.

To serve, use a knife or egg cutter to take the cap off the tip of the egg and eat it straight from the shell, preferably with plenty of toast for dipping. More firmly cooked eggs can be cracked (carefully!) and peeled like a hardboiled egg. All soft-boiled eggs should be cooked to order and eaten immediately.

Note: Hard-boiled eggs will cook through in 12 to 15 minutes after the whistle sounds.

CHAPTER 6

Pasta, Rice & Whole Grains

There is an exception to the rule of waterless cooking; pasta, whole grains and rice must be cooked in rapidly boiling Carico purified water so that individual pieces can float freely. Otherwise, these foods will stick together and cook unevenly.

Foods made from grains (wheat, rice, and oats) help form the foundation of a nutritious diet. They provide vitamins, minerals, carbohydrates (starch and dietary fiber), and other substances that are important for good health. Grain products are low in fat, unless fat is added in the processing, preparation, or at the table. Whole grains differ from refined grains in the amount of fiber and nutrients they provide, so choose a variety of whole and enriched grains. Eating plenty of whole grains, such as whole wheat bread or steel cut oats as part of the healthful eating patterns described by these guidelines, may help protect you against many chronic diseases.

CHAPTER 7

Appetizers, Soups & Salads

"Hors d'oeuvres," sounds French, and it is as French as costly Burgundy wines, but don't let that intimidate you. Hors d'oeuvres (literally translated) means "before or outside the main work." So "work," in a culinary sense, is a dinner. And "before" is the period of time before the dinner is served. We will concentrate on the before aspect of hors d'oeuvres (or "appetizers" as many Americans prefer) along with soups and salads, which play a very important role in the ultimate success of any dinner, and is a topic for which many home cooks need an infusion of new ideas.

Sopa de Habas Mexicana.
Pinto Bean Soup
Serves: 12
Preparation Time: 1 hour 30 minutes
Equipment: 8 or 10-inch chef knife, cutting board, 6-quart (5.7 L) covered roaster/saucepan

1	pound dried pinto beans
3	medium onions, finely chopped
5	cloves garlic, minced
1	tablespoon olive oil
2	red bell peppers, seeded and chopped
1	tablespoon chili powder
2	teaspoons ground cumin
6	cups Carico purified water
½	pound chorizo sausage, sliced (optional)
1	32 ounce can tomatoes, chopped, or 2½ pounds fresh plum tomatoes skinned, seeded and chopped
2	cups chicken broth or homemade chicken stock
2	tablespoons tomato paste
2	fresh limes, juice of
½	cup fresh cilantro, chopped

Rinse beans with Carico purified water and soak overnight. Alternatively, rinse beans, cover with Carico purified water and bring to a boil over medium heat for 2 minutes. Remove from heat and let soak 1 hour.

In the 6-quart (5.7 L) roaster/saucepan, over medium heat, sauté onions and garlic in olive oil until softened. Add red peppers, chili powder and cumin.

Drain soaked beans and add to 6-quart (5.7 L) roaster/saucepan with 6 cups Carico purified water. Cover, open the Ultra-Temp™ control and whistle valve, and reduce to medium-low heat for 1 hour. If using chorizo sausage, brown and drain on paper towels. Add chorizo sausage, tomatoes, chicken stock and tomato paste to soup, simmer 20 to 30 minutes or until heated through.

To serve, add 1 teaspoon of lime juice to individual serving bowls, ladle soup into bowls and top with cilantro.

NUTRITIONAL BREAKDOWN PER SERVING: Calories 133; Fat Grams 10; Carbohydrate Grams 20; Protein Grams 12; Cholesterol Grams 5; Sodium Grams 351 (178 if homemade chicken stock and fresh tomatoes).

Insalata di Broccoli

Broccoli Italian Style

Serves: 4

Preparation Time: 1 hour 15 minutes

Equipment: 8 or 10-inch chef knife, 2-quart (1.9 L) covered saucepan, mixing bowl and whisk

1	large head broccoli, broken in florets
1	teaspoon chopped fresh parsley
½	teaspoon freshly ground pepper

DRESSING

1	egg yolk, slightly beaten
3	tablespoons Carico purified water
2	teaspoons olive oil
3	tablespoons balsamic vinegar
1	teaspoon fresh lemon juice
¼	teaspoon freshly ground black pepper
1	teaspoon Dijon mustard
3	cloves garlic, finely minced
4	leaves Boston lettuce or romaine lettuce
2	ripe plum tomatoes, cut in 8 wedges
20	black olives
½	cup Romano cheese, grated

Place the broccoli in the saucepan, stem side down, making sure pan is nearly full. Rinse with Carico purified water and pour most of the water off. The water that clings to the broccoli and the little left in the pan is sufficient for cooking the waterless way.

Cover the pan, open the Ultra-Temp™ control and whistle valve and cook over medium heat. When the whistle sounds the Ultra-Temp™ temperature gauge should register between 160-195°F (71-91°C), (in the center of the cooking range). Close the whistle valve, spin the cover to form the vapor seal, and reduce to low heat. Broccoli will cook in 5 to 7 minutes per quart after the vapor seal is formed.

In a mixing bowl, whisk together the egg yolk, water, olive oil, balsamic vinegar, lemon juice, pepper, mustard and garlic. Continue whisking while gradually blending in the oil.

Chill the broccoli, salad dressing, tomato and lettuce in the refrigerator before serving, about 45 minutes to 1 hour.

To serve, place the lettuce on a salad plate, arranging the broccoli and tomato wedges on the lettuce. Top with salad dressing, black olives and grated cheese.

NUTRITIONAL BREAKDOWN PER SERVING: Calories 42; Fat Grams 2.7; Carbohydrate Grams 4.1; Protein Grams 1.5; Cholesterol mg 27; Sodium mg 76.

NOTE: Anyone who is ill, has a compromised immune system, the very young and the elderly, should avoid raw eggs because they may contain salmonella. Pasteurized raw eggs are available in some markets and are safe to use.

Southern Style Turkey Meatballs

Makes: 25-30 meatballs
Preparation Time: 50 minutes
Equipment: 8 or 10-inch chef knife, cutting board, 11-inch covered
fry/sauté skillet, mixing bowl

½	cup rolled oats
½	cup milk or almond milk
1	pound ground turkey or beef
2	medium sweet onions, minced
1	clove garlic, minced
1	tablespoon tomato paste
1	cup brewed coffee
¼	cup apple cider vinegar
2	tablespoons Worcestershire sauce
½	cup brown sugar
¼	teaspoon Dijon mustard
¼	teaspoon ground cinnamon
¼	cup ketchup
1	teaspoon chopped fresh parsley

In a mixing bowl, combine the oats and milk and let stand 15 to 20 minutes. Add the ground turkey and one of the minced onions. Mix well and form into 1-inch meatballs.

In a hot, dry skillet, dry sauté meatballs over medium heat until brown on all sides, about 15 minutes. Turn occasionally as they release from the skillet. Remove the meatballs with a slotted spoon and set aside.

Add the remaining onion and garlic to the skillet and sauté in the meatball drippings until slightly browned, 3 to 5 minutes, stirring occasionally. Add the tomato paste and sauté until it turns a reddish-brown color. Do not allow the residue that forms on the surface of the pan to burn.

To deglaze the pan, slowly stir in the coffee. Add the remaining ingredients, except for the parsley, and mix well.

Return the meatballs to the skillet. Cover and open the Ultra-Temp™ control and whistle valve. When the whistle sounds, close the whistle valve and reduce to low heat. Spin the cover to form the Ultra-Seal™. The Ultra-

Temp™ temperature gauge should read between 160-195°F (71-91°C). Simmer for 12 to 15 minutes.

To serve, sprinkle the meatballs with parsley and serve with cocktail forks or toothpicks.

NUTRITIONAL BREAKDOWN PER MEATBALL, WITH TURKEY: Calories 47; Fat Grams 1.4; Carbohydrate Grams 5.4; Protein Grams 3.3; Cholesterol mg 12; Sodium mg 55.

NUTRITIONAL BREAKDOWN PER MEATBALL, WITH BEEF: Calories 64; Fat Grams 3.3; Carbohydrate Grams 5.4; Protein Grams 3.3; Cholesterol mg 12; Sodium mg 52.

Italian Wedding Soup

Serves: 8
Preparation Time: 40 minutes
Equipment: 8 or 10-inch chef knife, mixing bowl, 11-inch gourmet skillet,
5-quart (4.7 L) roaster/saucepan

MEATBALLS
½   pound extra lean ground beef
1   teaspoon fresh basil, chopped
2   cloves garlic, minced
2   tablespoons tomato paste
½   cup Italian bread crumbs
1   egg

SOUP
8   cups chicken broth or homemade chicken stock
3   eggs, lightly beaten
1   cup Pastina (tiny stars) pasta
4   cups whole fresh spinach leaves

In mixing bowl, combine beef, basil, garlic, tomato paste, bread crumbs and egg, mix well and form into (16 to 20) small meatballs.

Preheat gourmet skillet over medium to medium-high heat and brown meatballs. Remove with a slotted spoon to paper towel to drain.

In the 5-quart (4.7 L) roaster/saucepan, add chicken stock and bring to a boil over medium heat. Stir in eggs gradually by swirling the soup as you pour in the lightly beaten eggs. This will prevent the eggs from scrambling in the hot liquid. Add pasta and simmer until pasta is cooked.

To serve, place 3-4 meatballs in individual soup bowls, add spinach leaves and pour soup mixture into bowl.

NUTRITIONAL BREAKDOWN PER SERVING: Calories 167; Fat Grams 8; Carbohydrate Grams 12; Protein Grams 12; Cholesterol mg 130; Sodium mg 230 (155 with homemade chicken stock).

Crab Stuffed Mushrooms

Serves: 12
Preparation Time: 20 minutes
Equipment: 8 or 10-inch chef knife, cutting board, mixing bowl, 11-inch covered fry/sauté skillet

2	cloves garlic, minced or pureed with a knife
¼	medium onion, minced
1	tablespoon fresh parsley, chopped
½	cup Swiss cheese, shredded
1	6-ounce can crab meat, (or freshly cooked)
12	large mushroom caps, cleaned and stems removed
½	teaspoon paprika
2-3	tablespoons Chardonnay wine or other dry white wine

In a mixing bowl, combine garlic, onions, parsley, cheese and crab meat. Set aside. Clean mushrooms by brushing with a soft cloth or paper towel. Do not rinse under water. Stuff the mushrooms with the crab meat mixture.

Place stuffed mushrooms in the 11-inch fry/sauté skillet, add 2 to 3 tablespoons of wine or Carico purified water, cover, open the Ultra-Temp™ control and whistle valve and cook over medium heat. When the whistle valve sounds the Ultra-Temp™ temperature gauge should register between 160-195°F (71-91°C), (in the center of the cooking range). Close the whistle valve and reduce the heat to low. Spin the cover to create the Ultra-Seal™ and cook for 10 to 12 minutes.

To serve, remove from skillet with slotted spoon and place on serving plate. Sprinkle with paprika.

NUTRITIONAL BREAKDOWN PER SERVING: Calories 43; Fat Grams 3; Carbohydrate Grams 2; Protein Grams 4; Cholesterol mg 15; Sodium mg 160.

Pasta é Faggioli
Italian Bean Soup "Pasta Fazool"
Serves: 8 to 10
Preparation Time: 40 minutes
Equipment: 8 or 10-inch chef knife, cutting board, 6-quart (5.7 L) covered roaster/saucepan

1	medium onion, minced
1	medium carrot, diced
1	stalk celery, diced
1	medium green bell pepper, seeded and diced
2	cloves garlic, minced
3	cups low-sodium chicken stock
4	cups cooked white (cannellini) beans in liquid, or 4 cups canned beans, not drained
1	teaspoon Italian seasoning
¼	cups tagliatelle or ditalini pasta
1	teaspoon distilled white vinegar
2	tablespoons freshly grated Parmesan cheese
4	fresh basil leaves, cut in ¼-inch strips

In a hot, dry pan over medium-high heat, dry sauté onion, carrot, celery, bell pepper and garlic until slightly browned and tender, about 7 to 10 minutes, stirring occasionally.

Slowly stir in the chicken stock. Add the beans, Italian seasoning, pasta and vinegar. Reduce to low heat. Cover the pan and open the Ultra-Temp™ control and whistle valve. The Ultra-Temp™ temperature gauge should read between 160-195°F (71-91°C). Simmer for 20 minutes. Do not allow soup to boil.

To serve, ladle the soup into soup bowls or a tureen and sprinkle with the basil and grated Parmesan cheese. Serve with warm Italian bread.

NUTRITIONAL BREAKDOWN PER SERVING: Calories 106; Fat Grams 1; Carbohydrate Grams 9; Protein Grams 9; Cholesterol Grams 1; Sodium Grams 392 (about 190 if homemade chicken stock).

Turchia Zuppa Italiana
Italian Turkey Soup
Serves: 10 to 12
Preparation Time: 30 minutes
Equipment: 8 or 10-inch chef knife, 9-inch gourmet skillet, 5-quart (4.7 L) covered roaster/saucepan

1	medium onion, diced
1	medium carrot, diced
2	stalks celery, diced
1	medium red bell pepper, seeded and diced
1	clove garlic, minced
6	cups low-sodium chicken stock
1	teaspoon poultry seasoning
1	pound turkey dark meat, skinless, cubed
1	cup fresh or frozen peas
8	ounces spinach-filled tortellini
1	tablespoon chopped fresh parsley

In a hot, dry 5-quart roaster/saucepan (4.7 L) over medium heat, dry sauté the onion, carrot, celery, bell pepper and garlic until slightly browned, about 5 to 7 minutes, stirring occasionally.

Slowly stir in the chicken stock. Add the remaining ingredients, except the parsley, and reduce to low heat. Cover the pan and open the Ultra-Temp™ control and whistle valve. Simmer until the turkey is tender, about 20 minutes. Do not allow the soup to boil or the temperature gauge to exceed 195°F (91°C).

To serve, ladle into soup bowls or a tureen and sprinkle with the parsley. Serve with warm Italian bread.

NUTRITIONAL BREAKDOWN PER SERVING: Calories 110; Fat Grams 3; Carbohydrate Grams 8; Protein Grams 16; Cholesterol mg 51; Sodium mg 392 (175 with homemade chicken stock).

Buffalo Chicken Wings

Makes: 48 appetizers
Preparation Time: 30 minutes
Equipment: 8 or 10-inch chef knife, kitchen shears, mixing bowls, 11-inch covered fry/sauté skillet

24	large chicken wings
4	stalks celery
1	cup low-sodium chicken stock
2	tablespoons hot sauce
¼	cup Italian bread crumbs

DIPPING SAUCE
½	cup sour cream
¼	cup crumbled blue cheese
¼	teaspoon Worcestershire sauce
¼	teaspoon hot sauce
¼	teaspoon Dijon mustard

With the chef knife or kitchen shears, trim off the tip of the chicken wings and discard. Cut the wings in half at the joint and trim the skin from the meat.

Begin with chicken that is nearly room temperature. To sear, preheat skillet over medium heat with the cover on and the whistle valve closed, about 4 to 5 minutes. When the Ultra-Temp™ temperature gauge registers close to 195°F (91°C), the pan is hot enough to begin the searing process. Remove the cover and place the chicken wings in the pan, pressing against the bottom to brown evenly. Chicken will stick at first but will loosen when seared properly, about 3 to 5 minutes per side. Sear on all sides.

Meanwhile, prepare the dipping sauce. In a mixing bowl, combine the sour cream, blue cheese, Worcestershire sauce, hot sauce and Dijon mustard.

With a knife, cut each celery stalk into 3 or 4 equal-size portions and then slice each portion into 3 or 4 bite-size sticks. Place the dipping sauce in the middle of a serving platter and arrange the celery sticks around the sauce.

Slowly stir the stock in with the chicken wings, and reduce to low heat. Add the hot sauce and bread crumbs and mix well. Stir until mixture thickens, 2 to 3 minutes.

To serve, remove the wings and bread crumb gravy to a warm platter. Serve with the celery sticks and dipping sauce.

NUTRITIONAL BREAKDOWN PER SERVING: Calories 47; Fat Grams 1.3; Carbohydrate Grams 0.5; Protein Grams 8; Cholesterol mg 20; Sodium mg 44.

CHAPTER 8

Beef, Pork & Poultry

NOTE: When cooking beef, pork and poultry, upon removing from the pan, do not cut into it immediately as the liquid will pool out and will end up dry. By letting it rest for 3 to 4 minutes, the moisture is redistributed and your meat will be tender and juicy.

Pollo y Ajo Asado
Chicken with Roasted Garlic
Serves: 6
Time: 50 minutes
Equipment: 8 or 10-inch chef knife, 11-inch covered fry/sauté skillet

3	pounds bone-in chicken pieces, skinned
40	cloves of garlic, unpeeled (about 4 bulbs)
1½	cups dry white wine
¼	teaspoon (4 sprigs) fresh thyme
¼	teaspoon (1 sprig) rosemary
2	tablespoons Cognac
1	tablespoon fresh parsley, chopped

Begin with chicken that is nearly room temperature. To sear, preheat skillet over medium heat, with the cover on the whistle valve closed, about 3 to 5 minutes. When the Ultra-Temp temperature gauge registers between 160-195°F (71-91°C), the pan is hot enough to begin searing the chicken. Remove the cover and place the chicken in the pan. Cover the pan and leave the lid slightly ajar. When the chicken loosens, about 5 to 7 minutes, turn to brown on the other side, about 4 to 5 minutes. Test for doneness by inserting the Ultra-Temp™ temperature gauge into the center of the breast. A safe internal temperature for chicken is 165°F (71°C). Transfer chicken to platter.

Add the unpeeled garlic cloves to the skillet and continue stirring for 3 to 5 minutes until garlic begins to brown. Return the chicken pieces to the pan. Add the wine, thyme and rosemary. Cover, reduce to low heat and simmer for 20 to 25 minutes.

Drizzle Cognac over chicken, cover and simmer about 5 minutes with the cover off.

To serve, remove the chicken pieces to a serving platter, surround with roasted garlic cloves, top with chopped parsley and serve with toasted Italian bread. When garlic is squeezed out of its natural wrapper, it spreads like butter on the bread.

NUTRITIONAL BREAKDOWN PER SERVING: Calories 250; Fat Grams 6; Carbohydrate Grams 18; Protein Grams 22; Cholesterol mg 58; Sodium mg 251.

Boeuf Bourguignon
Beef Stew
Serves: 8
Preparation Time: 2½ hours
Equipment: 8 or 10-inch chef knife, cutting board, 6-quart (5.7 L) covered
roaster/saucepan, 9-inch gourmet skillet

2	pounds sirloin steak cut in ¼-inch cubes
3	shallots, peeled and chopped
3	cloves garlic, chopped
2	tablespoons unbleached flour, or rice flour
3	cups dry red wine
1	bay leaf
2	cups low sodium beef stock, heated
1	teaspoon fresh basil, chopped
1	teaspoon fresh parsley, chopped
2	tablespoons unsalted butter
24	pearl onions, peeled
1	pound fresh mushrooms, cleaned and halved

Begin with steak that is nearly room temperature. Preheat 6-quart (5.7 L) roaster/saucepan over medium heat with the cover on and the whistle valve closed, about 3 to 4 minutes. When temperature gauge registers between 160-195°F (71-91°C), the pan is hot enough to begin searing the meat. Remove the cover, place steak in pan and brown evenly. Sirloin will loosen when seared properly, about 3 to 5 minutes per side. Add shallots and garlic, sauté 5 minutes. Dust meat with flour, stirring to combine ingredients, sauté 4 to 5 minutes.

Add wine to deglaze pan. Add bay leaf and bring to a simmer. Cook uncovered until liquid is reduced by half. Add beef stock, basil and parsley. Cover, open the Ultra-Temp™ control and whistle valve, reduce to low heat and simmer 2 hours.

Thirty minutes before serving, heat butter in skillet over low heat. Add pearl onions and mushrooms, sauté about 5 minutes, then add to stew.

To serve, remove bay leaf, ladle into individual serving bowls, top with parsley leaves and serve with toasted Italian or French garlic bread.

NUTRITIONAL BREAKDOWN PER SERVING: Calories 345; Fat Grams 6; Carbohydrate Grams 14; Protein Grams 50; Cholesterol mg 50; Sodium mg 847 (508 with homemade beef stock).

Marinated Round Steak with Broccoli

Serves: 6

Preparation Time: 1 hour 15 minutes

Equipment: 8 or 10-inch chef knife, cutting board, Carico 1650 ml (56 oz.) Ultra-Vac™, 3-quart mixing bowl, paring knife, 1-quart mixing bowl, 11-inch covered fry/sauté skillet

1	tablespoon dry sherry
2	teaspoons cornstarch
½	teaspoon sugar
1	teaspoon olive oil
1	teaspoon soy sauce
3	pounds lean round steak
1	pound fresh broccoli
1	tablespoon cornstarch
1	tablespoon dry sherry
½	cup homemade chicken stock, or chicken broth
1	tablespoon hoisin sauce
½	teaspoon sugar
1	teaspoon soy sauce
½	teaspoon ground white pepper
1	tablespoon olive oil
1	tablespoon ginger, freshly grated
2	cloves garlic, minced
1	medium sweet red pepper, seeded and cut into julienne strips
1	tablespoon toasted sesame seeds

In Carico Ultra-Vac™ container, combine 1 tablespoon dry sherry, 2 teaspoons cornstarch, ½ teaspoon sugar, 1 teaspoon olive oil, 1 teaspoon soy sauce and mix well. Add steak and toss gently. Cover, pump the air out of the Ultra-Vac™ to quick marinate, and refrigerate 1 hour or overnight.

With a paring knife, trim broccoli and remove tough ends of lower stalks. Cut off florets, set aside. Slice stalks in ¼-inch strips, set aside.

In small mixing bowl, combine 1 tablespoon cornstarch and 1 tablespoon dry sherry, stir well. Add chicken stock, hoisin sauce, ½ teaspoon sugar, 1 teaspoon soy sauce and white pepper. Stir well and set aside.

Begin with round steak that is nearly room temperature. To sear, preheat skillet over medium to medium-high heat with the cover on and the whistle valve closed, about 3 to 5 minutes. When the Ultra-Temp™ temperature gauge registers between 165-190°F (71-91°C) the pan is hot enough to begin stir frying.

Remove the cover, add olive oil and allow to heat 1 minute. Add ginger and garlic, stir fry about 30 seconds. Add beef and marinade, stir fry 1 minute. Add broccoli and red pepper; stir fry 2 to 3 minutes to desired doneness.

Add cornstarch mixture and continue to stir. Reduce heat to low, cover with Ultra-Temp™ control with whistle valve open, and cook 2 minutes or until whistle sounds and mixture slightly thickens.

To serve, spoon beef with broccoli over rice and sprinkle with sesame seeds.

NUTRITIONAL BREAKDOWN PER SERVING: Calories 343; Fat Grams 9; Carbohydrate Grams 36; Protein Grams 31; Cholesterol mg 64; Sodium mg 348 (209 with homemade Chicken Stock).

Fajitas de Carne

Serves: 12
Preparation Time: 1 hour, 15 minutes
Equipment: 8 or 10-inch chef knife, large Ultra-Vac™ container, 13-inch gourmet skillet

MARINADE

4	cloves garlic, minced and mashed into a paste
¼	cup fresh squeezed lime juice
1½	teaspoons ground cumin
2	tablespoons olive oil

FAJITAS

2	pounds flank steak
2	tablespoons olive oil
3	assorted colored bell peppers, sliced thin
1	large red onion, sliced thin
2	garlic cloves, minced
12	7-inch flour tortillas, warmed

In the large Ultra-Vac™ container, prepare marinade by combining garlic paste, lime juice, cumin and olive oil. Place the flank steak in the Ultra-Vac™ container, cover, lock and shake. Pump the air out, and chill in the refrigerator for at least 1 hour or overnight.

To grill the steak, preheat the 13-inch gourmet skillet over medium-high heat. Add whole steak to pan and sear. When it releases easily from the pan, turn and sear the other side. Test for doneness, according to the chart below, by inserting the Ultra-Tech™ temperature gauge into the center of meat. Remove the steak to a warm platter and keep warm. Remove the skillet from the heat and allow to cool.

Rare (red 145°F) approximately 3 to 4 minutes per side

Medium Rare (dark pink 150°F) 4 to 5 minutes per side

Medium (light pink 160°F) 5 to 6 minutes per side

Well-done (dry 170°F) approximately 6 to 7 minutes per side

Reheat the 13-inch skillet over medium heat until it is hot but not smoking. Add the bell peppers, onion and garlic. Sauté the mixture, stirring occasionally until the bell peppers are softened, 5 to 7 minutes.

To serve, slice the steak thin across the grain on a diagonal bias and arrange slices on serving platter. Top with bell pepper mixture and serve with tortillas.

NUTRITIONAL BREAKDOWN PER SERVING: Calories 542; Fat Grams 21; Carbohydrate Grams 46; Protein Grams 41; Cholesterol mg 75; Sodium mg 394.

Beefy Macaroni Casserole

Serves: 6
Preparation Time: 45 minutes
Equipment: 8 or 10-inch chef knife, 11-inch covered fry/sauté skillet

½	pound lean ground beef or ground turkey
1	green pepper, seeded and chopped fine
1	onion, chopped
1	cup celery, diced
¼	teaspoon Worcestershire sauce
¼	teaspoon pepper
1½	cups tomato juice or V8
1	cup elbow macaroni, uncooked
½	cup mushrooms, sliced
1	tablespoon parsley, chopped

Preheat covered skillet for 4 to 5 minutes over medium to medium-high heat. When the Ultra-Temp™ temperature gauge registers between 160-195°F (71-91°C) the skillet is hot enough to sear the meat and lock in the natural juices. Remove the cover and add the ground beef to the hot, dry pan. Stir and separate to cover the entire bottom of the pan. Cover and cook 4-5 minutes.

Add green pepper, onions and celery. Reduce to medium heat and cover, leaving the lid slightly ajar, and cook 8 to 10 minutes, stirring occasionally.

Add remaining ingredients, reduce the heat to low, cover and close the Ultra-Temp™ control and whistle valve. The optimum cooking temperature should read about 160°F (71°C). Simmer 15 to 20 minutes.

To serve, spoon into individual serving bowls, top with fresh chopped parsley.

NUTRITIONAL BREAKDOWN PER SERVING: Calories 139; Fat Grams 5; Carbohydrate Grams 15; Protein Grams 9; Cholesterol mg 23; Sodium mg 238.

Baked Lemon Chicken

Serves: 4

Time: 40 minutes

Equipment: 8 or 10-inch chef knife, cutting board, 11-inch covered fry/sauté skillet, 1-quart mixing bowl

4	chicken breast halves, skinless
3	tablespoon fresh squeezed lemon juice
2	tablespoons Carico purified water
¼	teaspoon onion powder
¼	teaspoon marjoram leaves
¼	teaspoon sea salt or kosher salt
¼	teaspoon paprika
1	tablespoon fresh parsley
	chopped lemon and orange slices

Begin with chicken breasts that are nearly room temperature. To sear, preheat skillet over medium heat, with the cover on and the whistle valve closed, about 3 to 5 minutes. When the Ultra-Temp™ temperature gauge registers between 160-195°F (71-91°C) the pan is hot enough to begin searing the chicken. Remove the cover and place the chicken in the pan, pressing against the bottom to brown evenly. Poultry will stick at first but will loosen when seared properly, about 7 to 8 minutes per side. Turn and sear on the other side. Test for doneness by inserting Ultra-Temp™ temperature gauge into the center of the chicken breast. The USDA recommended safe internal temperature for chicken is 165°F (74°C).

In the small mixing bowl, combine all other ingredients, except parsley, and pour over browned chicken. Cover with the whistle valve closed, reduce the heat to low and simmer 15 minutes.

To serve, remove chicken to individual serving plates, garnish with parsley lemon and orange slices. Serve with snow peas and toasted sesame seeds.

NUTRITIONAL BREAKDOWN PER SERVING: Calories 298; Fat Grams 6; Carbohydrate Grams 4; Protein Grams 54; Cholesterol mg 146; Sodium mg 261.

Roasted Rosemary Chicken

Serves: 4-6
Time: 1 hour, 20 minutes
Equipment: 8 or 10-inch chef knife, cutting board, 6-quart (5.7 L)
roaster/saucepan with large dome cover

1   whole chicken
3   sprigs fresh rosemary
½   stick unsalted butter, softened or ¼ cup olive oil
2   cups low sodium chicken broth
¼   cup white wine
1   tablespoon cornstarch
1   tablespoon Carico purified water

Clean chicken with Carico purified water, pat dry and place one whole sprig of rosemary in the cavity and one in the fold of each wing, next to the breast. (Tie chicken with string to keep rosemary in place and wings tucked.) Baste chicken with butter or olive oil.

Place chicken on its side in 6-quart (5.7 L) roaster/saucepan. Cover and roast for 30 minutes over medium-low heat. Turn the chicken to the other side, cover, and roast an additional 30 minutes. Turn chicken upright and roast an additional 20 minutes. Remove to a platter and keep warm

NOTE: Perfect roasting temperature is when the dome cover spins on a cushion of water emitting tiny bubbles. If it spits moisture, the heat is too high. Lower the heat.

To prepare gravy, increase heat to medium high and deglaze the stockpot with ¼ cup white wine and 2 cups low sodium chicken stock. Reduce liquid by half to thicken, or add 1 tablespoon cornstarch mixed with 1 tablespoon of Carico purified water or chicken stock to thicken.

To serve, slice chicken and serve with rice and gravy.

NUTRITIONAL BREAKDOWN PER SERVING: Calories 364; Fat Grams 25; Carbohydrate Grams 2; Protein Grams 31; Cholesterol mg 121; Sodium mg 84.

Turquía Pimienta Rellena
Turkey Stuffed Peppers
Serves: 6
Preparation Time: 50 minutes
Equipment: 8 or 10-inch chef knife, cutting board, 11-inch fry/sauté skillet,
large dome cover

1	onion, chopped
2	cloves garlic, minced
1	tablespoon olive oil
1½	pounds ground turkey
¾	cup cooked brown, yellow or white rice
2	7 ounce cans tomato sauce
4	tablespoons fresh parsley, chopped
6	bell peppers, assorted colors

In the 11-inch fry/sauté skillet, over medium heat, sauté onion and garlic in olive oil for 3 to 5 minutes. Add ground turkey and cook until turkey is no longer pink in color. Stir in cooked rice, tomato sauce and parsley, stirring occasionally. Set skillet aside to cool slightly.

Remove tops and seed peppers. Spoon turkey and rice mixture into bell peppers and stand peppers upright in large skillet. Spoon remaining sauce on top of peppers, and add 2 to 3 tablespoons of Carico purified water to skillet. Cover with large dome cover and cook waterless over medium-low heat to form a vapor seal. When the lid spins freely on a cushion of water the Ultra-Seal™ is formed. Cook through until tender, approximately 20 to 25 minutes.

NUTRITIONAL BREAKDOWN PER SERVING: Calories 320; Fat Grams 13; Carbohydrate Grams 26; Protein Grams 26; Cholesterol mg 90; Sodium mg 165.

Turkey with Orzo and Broccoli

Serves: 8
Preparation Time: 30 minutes
Equipment: chef knife, cutting board, 11-inch covered fry/sauté skillet

1	skinless turkey breast, cut into 1 inch strips, then halved
1	onion, sliced thin
3	cloves garlic, chopped
1	16 ounce can chopped tomatoes or 1½ pounds plum tomatoes, peeled, seeded and chopped
1½	cups uncooked orzo pasta
2	cups Carico purified water, or chicken broth
1	medium head fresh broccoli florets

Begin with turkey that is nearly room temperature. To sear, preheat skillet over medium heat with the cover on and the whistle valve closed, about 3 to 5 minutes. When the Ultra-Temp™ temperature gauge registers between 165-195°F (71-91°C), the pan is hot enough to begin searing the meat. Remove the cover and place the turkey breast strips in the pan, pressing against the bottom to brown evenly. Poultry will stick at first but will loosen when seared properly, about 4 to 5 minutes per side. Turn and sear on the other side.

Add onion and garlic and sauté 2 to 3 minutes. Reduce to low heat, add tomatoes and mix well. Push mixture to center of pan. Pour dried orzo around outside rim of pan, pour Carico purified water over orzo, cover, open the Ultra-Temp™ control and whistle valve, and cook 10 minutes. Top with broccoli, cover and cook about 5 to 7 minutes.

To serve, place hot 11-inch fry/sauté skillet on the inverted cover (with thermometer removed) and serve directly from pan.

NUTRITIONAL BREAKDOWN PER SERVING: Calories 165; Fat Grams 1; Carbohydrate Grams 14; Protein Grams 25; Cholesterol mg 64; Sodium mg 137.

Braised Breast of Duck
with Persimmons and Prunes

Serves: 4

Preparation Time: 30 minutes

Equipment: 8 or 10-inch chef knife, mixing bowl, cutting board, paring knife, 11-inch covered fry/sauté skillet

2	skinless duck breasts (about 4 to 5 ounces each)
1½	cups fresh squeezed orange juice
¼	cup packed light brown sugar
½	teaspoon ground cinnamon
1	persimmon, cut crosswise into ¼-inch slices
4	prunes, cut into ¼-inch-thick slices
1	tablespoon grated orange zest

Begin with duck that is nearly room temperature. To sear, preheat skillet over medium-high heat with the cover on and the whistle valve closed, about 3 to 5 minutes. When the Ultra-Temp™ temperature gauge registers close to 195°F (91°C), the pan is hot enough to sear the duck. Remove the cover and place the duck breasts in the pan, pressing against the bottom to brown evenly. Duck will stick at first but will loosen when seared properly, about 3 to 4 minutes. Turn and sear on the other side, about 3 to 4 minutes.

Do not overcook. Insert the Ultra-Temp™ temperature gauge into the center of the duck breast. Duck is best served rare at an internal temperature of 130-135°F (54-57°C). Transfer to warm platter to rest, keep warm.

Deglaze skillet with orange juice. Add brown sugar, cinnamon, persimmons and prunes. Reduce to medium-low heat and simmer 4 to 5 minutes. Return the duck to skillet. Cover and simmer 2 to 3 minutes. Transfer the duck to a cutting board and cut on a bias into ¼-inch-thick slices.

To serve, top the sliced duck with the sauce, persimmons and prunes. Sprinkle with the orange zest. Serve with crispy hash-brown cauliflower and candied carrots.

NUTRITIONAL BREAKDOWN PER SERVING: Calories 173; Fat Grams 3.6; Carbohydrate Grams 25; Protein Grams 11; Cholesterol mg 44; Sodium mg 46.

Southern Barbecued Chicken

Serves: 6 to 8
Preparation Time: 45 minutes
Equipment: Carico cleaver, cutting board, 11-inch covered fry/sauté skillet

2	skinless chicken legs
2	skinless chicken thighs
2	skinless chicken breast halves
2	medium sweet onions, diced
2	cloves garlic, minced
2	tablespoons tomato paste
2	cups fresh brewed coffee
½	cup apple cider vinegar
2	tablespoon Worcestershire sauce
1	cup packed light brown sugar
¼	teaspoon red pepper flakes
¼	teaspoon Dijon mustard
¼	teaspoon ground cinnamon (optional)
1	tablespoon minced fresh rosemary
1	tablespoon chopped fresh parsley

Cut up whole chicken with Carico cleaver or use pieces already cut.

Begin with chicken that is nearly room temperature. To sear, preheat skillet over medium heat with the cover on and the whistle valve closed, about 3 to 5 minutes. When the Ultra-Temp™ temperature gauge registers between 160-195°F (71-91°C), the pan is hot enough to begin searing the chicken. Remove the cover and place the chicken parts in the pan, pressing against the bottom to brown evenly. Poultry will stick at first but will loosen when seared properly, about 7 to 8 minutes per side. Turn and sear on the other side.

Test for doneness by inserting the Ultra-Temp™ temperature gauge into the center of the breast. The USDA recommended safe internal temperature for chicken is a minimum of 165°F (74°C). Remove the chicken to a warm platter and keep warm.

Add onion and garlic and sauté in the chicken drippings until slightly browned, 3 to 4 minutes, stirring occasionally. Add the tomato paste and stir until the paste turns a reddish-brown in color, about 5 minutes. Do not allow the residue that forms on the bottom of the pan to burn.

Slowly stir in the coffee. Add the remaining ingredients, except the parsley, and stir to combine. Return the chicken to the pan, and reduce to low heat. Cover the skillet, close the Ultra-Temp™ control and whistle valve and simmer for 10 to 15 minutes. Do not boil, or allow the temperature gauge to exceed the center of the optimum cooking range 160-195°F (71-91°C).

To serve, top the chicken with barbecue sauce, sprinkle with parsley and serve with baked beans and fresh corn on the cob cooked the waterless way.

NUTRITIONAL BREAKDOWN FOR SKINLESS CHICKEN, PER SERVING: Calories 238; Fat Grams 4; Carbohydrate Grams 23; Protein Grams 27; Cholesterol mg 89; Sodium mg 160.

Chicken Cacciatore

Serves: 8
Preparation Time: 45 minutes
Equipment: Carico cleaver, cutting board, 11-inch covered fry/sauté skillet,
6-quart roaster/saucepan

8	skinless chicken thighs
1	medium onion, diced
1	clove garlic, minced
1	medium carrot, diced
1	stalk celery, diced
2	tablespoons tomato paste
½	cup port wine
1	tablespoon Italian seasoning
½	teaspoon freshly ground black pepper
¼	teaspoon red pepper flakes (optional)
1	cup sliced fresh mushrooms (2 to 3 ounces)
1	cup low-sodium chicken stock
2	cups seeded and chopped plum tomatoes or canned whole peeled tomatoes
1	pound linguini pasta
2	tablespoons freshly grated Parmesan cheese
2	tablespoons chopped fresh basil

Begin with chicken thighs that are nearly room temperature. To sear, preheat skillet over medium heat with the cover on and the whistle valve closed, about 3 to 5 minutes. When the Ultra-Temp™ temperature gauge registers between 160-195°F (71-91°C), the pan is hot enough to begin searing the chicken. Remove the cover and place the thighs in the pan, pressing against the bottom to brown evenly. Chicken will stick at first but will loosen when seared properly, about 7 to 8 minutes per side. Turn and sear on the other side.

Test for doneness by inserting the Ultra-Temp™ temperature gauge into the center of the thigh. The USDA recommended safe internal temperature for chicken is a minimum of 165°F (74°C). Remove the chicken to a warm platter and keep warm.

Add the onion, garlic, carrot and celery and sauté in the chicken drippings until slightly browned, 3 to 4 minutes, stirring occasionally. Add the tomato paste and stir until the paste turns a reddish-brown in color, about 5 minutes. Do not allow the residue that forms on the bottom of the pan to burn.

Deglaze the pan with the port wine. Reduce the heat to low and simmer until reduced by half. Stir in the Italian seasoning, black pepper and red pepper.

Add the mushrooms, chicken stock and tomatoes. Mix well. Return the chicken thighs to the skillet and baste with sauce. Cover the pan, close the Ultra-Temp™ control and whistle valve and simmer 15 to 20 minutes. The temperature gauge should read directly between 160-195°F (71-91°C).

Meanwhile, in the 6-quart (5.7 L) roaster/saucepan cook the linguini according to package directions in 5-quarts of Carico purified water or almond milk.

To serve, divide the linguini among 8 serving plates and divide the sauce over the linguini. Place one chicken thigh on each serving. Sprinkle with the Parmesan cheese and top with chopped fresh basil.

NUTRITIONAL BREAKDOWN FOR SKINLESS CHICKEN PER SERVING WITH FRESH TOMATOES: Calories 270; Fat Grams 4.8; Carbohydrate Grams 29; Protein Grams 25; Cholesterol mg 79; Sodium mg 252 (canned tomatoes add 94mg sodium per serving).

VARIATION

For a Spanish flair, add 1 minced chorizo sausage link, ½ cup sliced black olives and 2 tablespoons of capers. Serve over yellow rice.

NUTRITIONAL BREAKDOWN PER SERVING: Calories 298; Fat Grams 8.7; Carbohydrate Grams 26; Protein Grams 25; Cholesterol mg 85; Sodium mg 455

Roast Stuffed Chicken
with Port Marinara

Serves: 6
Preparation Time: 45 minutes
Equipment: medium mixing bowl, 8 or 10-inch chef knife, cutting board,
paring knife, 13-inch gourmet skillet with tempered glass lid.

3	slices whole wheat, Italian or cornbread, crumbled
1	medium shallot, minced fine
1	stalk celery, minced fine
2	cloves garlic, minced and mashed into a paste
½	teaspoon poultry seasoning
6	skinless medium chicken breast halves
1	medium onion, diced
2	cloves garlic, sliced paper thin
2	tablespoons fresh oregano, chopped or 1 tablespoon dried
1	tablespoon tomato paste
½	cup good-quality port wine
2	cups seeded and chopped plum tomatoes or canned whole peeled tomatoes
1	tablespoon freshly grated Parmesan cheese
1	tablespoon chopped fresh basil

In a mixing bowl, combine the bread, shallots, celery, garlic and poultry seasoning. Mix the ingredients until combined and are moist and firm. Form into 6 equal portions. Set aside.

With a paring knife, make a pocket by inserting the knife into the side of the chicken breast between the rib cage and the meat. Place a portion of stuffing into the pocket of each chicken breast half.

Preheat the gourmet skillet over medium to medium-high heat, about 3 to 4 minutes. Place the chicken in the pan; it will stick at first while browning. Cover the pan leaving the cover slightly ajar. When the chicken loosens, about 7 to 8 minutes, turn it to brown on the other side. Remove the chicken to a warm platter and keep warm.

To the skillet, add onion and sliced garlic, sauté in the chicken drippings until slightly browned, 3 to 4 minutes, stirring occasionally. Add the oregano and tomato paste and cook, stirring until the paste turns a reddish-brown in color, about 5 minutes. Do not allow the residue that forms on the bottom of the pan to burn.

Slowly stir in the wine. Stir in the tomatoes and return the chicken to the sauce. Reduce the heat to low. Cover the pan and simmer 10 to 12 minutes.

To serve, top the chicken with the sauce and sprinkle with Parmesan cheese and chopped fresh basil. Serve with fresh mustard greens or spinach cooked the waterless way.

NUTRITIONAL BREAKDOWN PER SERVING WITH FRESH TOMATOES: Calories 254; Fat Grams 3; Carbohydrate Grams 15; Protein Grams 35; Cholesterol mg 83; Sodium mg 295.

CHAPTER 9

Seafood

Orange Roughy á la Asparagus

Serves: 8

Preparation Time: 25 minutes

Equipment: 8 or 10-inch chef knife, cutting board, 13-inch gourmet skillet with tempered glass cover, or electric skillet

1	pound fresh asparagus spears cut into 1-inch pieces
1	2 ounce jar pimientos, drained and diced
2	tablespoons fresh squeezed lemon juice
$\frac{1}{4}$	teaspoon dried whole thyme (or fresh)
$\frac{1}{4}$	teaspoon garlic powder
$\frac{1}{4}$	teaspoon fresh ground black pepper
3	pounds orange roughy fillets
2	tablespoons sliced toasted almonds
	ground pepper (optional)

In a mixing bowl, combine asparagus with pimientos, lemon juice, thyme, garlic and fresh ground pepper (optional). Set aside.

Arrange fillets in cool 13-inch gourmet skillet or electric skillet and spoon asparagus mixture over fillets. Cover, and cook over medium-low heat, 15 to 20 minutes until fish flakes easily when tested with fork.

To serve, top with sliced toasted almonds.

NUTRITIONAL BREAKDOWN PER SERVING: Calories 149; Fat Grams 2; Carbohydrate Grams 2; Protein Grams 29; Cholesterol mg 35; Sodium mg 178.

Georgia Catfish Barbecue

Serves: 6
Preparation Time: 50 minutes
Equipment: mixing bowl, 8 or 10-inch chef knife, cutting board, 11-inch
covered fry/sauté skillet, large Ultra-Vac™ cover

½   cup barbecue sauce or ketchup
1   tablespoon fresh squeezed lemon juice
1   teaspoon brown sugar
2   teaspoons olive oil
1   teaspoon Worcestershire sauce
½   teaspoon dried whole marjoram
¼   teaspoon garlic powder
¼   teaspoon ground red pepper
6   4 ounce catfish fillets

In the mixing bowl combine barbecue sauce, lemon juice, sugar, olive oil, Worcestershire sauce, marjoram, garlic powder and red pepper. Mix well.

Arrange fillets in the 11-inch fry/sauté skillet and spoon barbecue mixture over fillets. Cover with the Ultra-Vac™ universal lid, pump the air out and marinate in the skillet, in the refrigerator, 30 minutes to 1 hour, turning once. Remove Ultra-Vac™ lid.

Place 11-inch fry/sauté skillet over medium-low heat, and bring to a simmer. Cover and open the Ultra-Temp™ control and whistle valve. When the whistle sounds, close the whistle valve, reduce to low heat, and spin the cover to form the vapor seal. Cook 15 minutes or until fish flakes easily when tested with a fork.

To serve, remove catfish fillets to individual serving plates, drizzle with sauce and serve with warm green bean salad.

NUTRITIONAL BREAKDOWN PER SERVING: Calories 239; Fat Grams 14; Carbohydrate Grams 3; Protein Grams 25; Cholesterol mg 74; Sodium mg 193.

Saumon Poché Français

French Poached Salmon

Serves: 6

Preparation Time: 35 minutes

Equipment: 8 to 10-inch chef knife, cutting board, 11-inch covered fry/sauté skillet

4	cups Carico purified water
½	medium onion, chopped
1	small carrot, sliced
½	stalk celery, sliced
2	cloves garlic, minced
6	pepper corns
4	allspice, whole
1	Bouquet Garni*
2	tablespoons fresh squeezed lemon juice
1	pound salmon fillet
½	fresh lemon, sliced thin
3-4	sprigs fresh thyme

In the 11-inch fry/sauté skillet, combine all ingredients except salmon, lemon and thyme. Cover and open the Ultra-Temp control and whistle valve. Bring to a simmer over medium heat. When the whistle sounds reduce the heat to low for 5 minutes. Place fillet in skillet, leave the whistle valve open and continue to simmer, approximately 8 to 10 minutes.

To serve, remove fillet with a spatula to a serving platter, garnish with lemon slices, top with fresh thyme and serve with rice or fresh vegetables cooked the waterless way.

NUTRITIONAL BREAKDOWN PER SERVING: Calories 108; Fat Grams 3; Carbohydrate Grams 5; Protein Grams 16; Cholesterol mg 39; Sodium mg 73.

*BOUQUET GARNI: A mixture of herbs (tied by the stems or placed in a cloth bag) to flavor broth or stew and removed before serving. Traditional Bouquet Garni includes fresh parsley, fresh thyme and a dried bay leaf, tied together in a bunch.

Cozze al Vapore Vino Rosso
Mussels Steamed in Wine
Serves: 8
Preparation Time: 40 minutes
Equipment: 8 or 10-inch chef knife, cutting board, 5-quart (4.7 L) covered
roaster/saucepan

1	teaspoon olive oil
2	medium onions, minced fine
4	cloves garlic, minced fine
2	cups (480 ml) red wine
4	dozen mussels*

In the 5-quart roaster/saucepan (4.7 L), sauté onions and garlic in olive oil over medium heat until tender. Add wine and bring to a simmer. Add mussels, cover, open the Ultra-Temp™ control and whistle vent. When the whistle sounds, close the whistle valve and reduce heat to low, and spin the cover to form the Ultra-Seal™. Simmer for 5 to 7 minutes or until mussels open.

To serve, spoon into individual soup bowls, top with wine sauce and serve with garlic bread.

*Mussels need to breathe; remove mussels from bag as soon as possible. To clean mussels prior to cooking, submerge mussels in Carico purified water with 4 tablespoons of cornstarch for 30 minutes. Scrape off beards, rinse and soak again. Discard any mussels that open before cooking. Mussels that do not open after cooking should not be consumed.

NUTRITIONAL BREAKDOWN PER SERVING: Calories 190; Fat Grams 4; Carbohydrate Grams 10; Protein Grams 17; Cholesterol mg 63; Sodium mg 364.

Cozze in Brodo di Pomodoro

Mussels in Tomato Broth

Use white wine instead of red wine, and add:

1   32 ounce (920 g) can plum tomatoes, chopped or crushed
1   cup fresh parsley leaves, chopped
2   teaspoons dried oregano
1-2   tablespoons, hot crushed red pepper flakes (optional)

Simmer 15 minutes before adding mussels.

Nutritional breakdowns not included for this variation.

Paella de Valencia

Serves: 16

Preparation Time: 45 minutes

Equipment: Carico shears, 8 or 10-inch chef knife, cutting board, 13-inch gourmet skillet with tempered glass cover

2	tablespoons olive oil
2	pounds chicken wings, wingtips trimmed then cut in half at joint with Carico shears
1	pound chorizo sausage, sliced
1/4	pound lean pork, cubed
1/4	pound pre-cooked ham, cubed
3	onions, chopped
2	green peppers, seeded and chopped
4	cloves garlic, minced
3	fresh tomatoes, quartered and seeded
1	teaspoon oregano
5	cups Carico purified water
2	cups uncooked yellow rice
1/4	teaspoon saffron
1	pound cooked shrimp
1/2	pound cooked lobster, cubed
1	10 ounce package frozen peas
1	32 ounce can artichoke hearts, drained
16	clams or mussels*
1	4 ounce can pimientos, sliced

Preheat 13-inch gourmet skillet over medium-high heat, about 2 to 3 minutes. Add the oil and heat 1 to 2 minutes. Add the chicken, chorizo, pork and ham, and sauté until browned. Add onions, peppers and garlic, sauté 3 to 5 minutes until tender. Add the tomatoes, oregano, water, rice and saffron. Mix well, cover and reduce to medium-low heat. Simmer 15 to 20 minutes. Arrange the shrimp, lobster, peas, artichokes, pimientos and mussels (clams) over the rice. Cover, cook 15 to 20 minutes or until rice is cooked through and mussels have opened.

To serve, bring to table and serve from the pan.

*Mussels and clams need to breathe; remove them from bag as soon as possible. To clean mussels or clams prior to cooking, submerge them in Carico purified water with 4 tablespoons of cornstarch for 30 minutes. If using mussels, scrape off beards. Rinse and soak again. Discard any mussels

or clams that open before cooking. Mussels or clams that do not open after cooking should not be consumed.

NOTE: *In Spain and in Spanish communities worldwide there are hundreds of authentic Paella recipes, typically dictated by fresh ingredients available in the region. Olive oil, saffron and rice are typically the common ingredients in all Paella recipes.*

NUTRITIONAL BREAKDOWN PER SERVING: Calories 341; Fat Grams 16; Carbohydrate Grams 25; Protein Grams 26; Cholesterol mg 96; Sodium mg 656.

CHAPTER 10

Vegetables

Minerals and vitamins are water and grease soluble. When you boil, steam, pressure cook in water, or microwave vegetables, you dissolve out the minerals and vitamins. Internal temperatures above 160°F (71°C) destroy life-giving enzymes. Ultra-Tech II™ waterless cookware, with our exclusive Ultra-Temp™ control and patented whistle valve and temperature gauge, is designed to cook your vegetables in a controlled environment, producing healthier meals while preserving more nutrients than any other cookware on the planet today.

Medley of Vegetables

Serves: 2
Preparation Time: 25 minutes
Equipment: chef knife, 1.7-quart (1.6 L) covered saucepan/sauté skillet

2	red potatoes, quartered or cut in half with skin on
2	carrots, sliced
6-8	broccoli florets
1	ear of corn, cut in half
1	wedge red or green cabbage, cut in half

One big advantage of using Ultra-Tech II™ cookware is the ability to cook more than one vegetable in the same pan, at the same time, without the loss of valuable nutrients, and with no interchanging of flavors or colors; and the vegetables taste great too!

First, place dense root vegetables such as potatoes and carrots on the bottom of the pan, then fill the pan with broccoli, corn and cabbage. Rinse with Carico purified water and pour most of the water off. The water that clings to the vegetables is sufficient to cook the waterless way. Cover the pan with the Ultra-Temp™ control with whistle valve open and place the pan over medium heat. When the whistle sounds the temperature gauge should register between 160-195°F (71-91°C), in the center of the cooking range of the thermometer. Close the whistle valve and reduce the heat to low to create a vapor seal (Ultra-Seal™). The vapor seal is formed when the lid spins freely on a cushion of moisture. Begin timing the vegetables. A medley of vegetables will cook in 10 to 15 minutes per quart; 10 minutes for crispy cooked and 15 minutes for soft and cooked through.

NUTRITIONAL BREAKDOWN PER SERVING: Calories 110; Fat Grams 1.5; Carbohydrate Grams 11; Protein Grams 1; Cholesterol mg 0; Sodium mg 35.

Vegetable Stir Fry

Serves: 8

Preparation Time: 25 minutes

Equipment: 8 or 10-inch chef knife, cutting board, electric skillet or 11-inch covered fry/sauté skillet

2	teaspoons sesame oil
2	cups broccoli florets cut into 1-inch (2.5 cm) pieces
2	large carrots, sliced
2	zucchini, chopped
2	red onions, chopped
2	tablespoons white wine
1	cup fresh mushrooms, sliced
1	teaspoon fresh dill, chopped
4	plum tomatoes, halved

Cover the 11-inch fry/sauté skillet with the Ultra-Temp™ control with whistle valve open and place the pan over medium-high heat. When the Ultra-Temp™ thermometer registers about 210°F (99°C) in the "red", uncover the pan and add the oil.

Add vegetables and cook, tossing quickly and constantly until they are crisp and tender, about 3 to 4 minutes. The quick cooking will seal in the fresh flavor, juices and valuable nutrients.

When stir-frying a mixture of vegetables, place longer cooking vegetables in the skillet and partially cook before adding the tenderer, quick cooking vegetables. For slightly softer vegetables, cover the pan and reduce to low heat for the final minutes of cooking.

NUTRITIONAL BREAKDOWN PER SERVING: Calories 70; Fat Grams 3; Carbohydrate Grams 11; Protein Grams 2; Cholesterol mg 0; Sodium mg 159.

Eggplant Parmigiana

Serves: 8

Preparation Time: 1 hour

Equipment: 10-inch chef knife, 13-inch gourmet skillet, 11-inch covered fry/sauté skillet, 8-inch scalloped knife

3	medium eggplants, sliced into ½-inch rings
2	tablespoons olive oil
3	cups (720 ml) Marinara sauce (see next page)
2	cups mushrooms, sliced thin
3	cups mozzarella cheese, shredded
¼	cup Romano cheese, grated
4-6	leaves fresh basil, chopped or julienne sliced

Slice eggplants to desired thickness and sprinkle with kosher salt. Make several small stacks of the sliced eggplant, placing a paper towel between each slice. Place something heavy, such as a large skillet or a heavy book on top of the stacks of eggplant rings. Press about 20 to 30 minutes, rinse in Carico purified water and pat dry. By salting and pressing, any bitterness present in the eggplant is removed.

Preheat 13-inch gourmet skillet over medium heat, add olive oil and bring to temperature. Add enough eggplant rings to fill pan, fry both sides until golden brown and remove to paper towels to drain.

Cover the bottom of the 11-inch fry/sauté skillet with a layer of Marinara sauce. Place one layer of eggplant across the bottom, layer with a mixture of mushrooms and mozzarella cheese, top with a layer of Marinara sauce, then repeat the process. Finish top layer with mozzarella and sprinkle with Romano cheese. Cover, close the Ultra-Temp™ control and whistle valve, and cook over low heat for 30 to 35 minutes.

To serve, remove from heat and let stand 10 to 15 minutes. Using the Carico 8-inch scalloped utility knife, slice into 8 individual servings. Top with fresh basil and serve.

NUTRITIONAL BREAKDOWN PER SERVING: Calories 226; Fat Grams 13; Carbohydrate Grams 11; Protein Grams 18; Cholesterol mg 39; Sodium mg 906.

Marinara Sauce

Serves: 12 – 1 cup servings
Yields: 2-quarts (2 L)
Equipment: 8 or 10-inch chef knife, cutting board, 5-quart (4.7 L)
roaster/saucepan

2	tablespoons olive oil
½	medium onion, chopped
1	12 ounce can tomato paste
½	cup red wine
3	cups Carico purified water
1	tablespoon dried basil
1	tablespoon dried oregano
2	tablespoons fresh parsley, chopped
1	14.5 ounce can diced tomatoes, or 1¼ pounds plum tomatoes, peeled, seeded and diced

In the 5-quart (4.7 L) roaster/saucepan sauté onion in olive oil over medium heat until tender, about 5 minutes. Add tomato paste and fry until tomato paste turns Indian red. Tomato paste will leave a sugar residue on bottom of pan; stir continuously to prevent from sticking or burning. Deglaze the pan with wine and cook down until sauce thickens and alcohol is cooked off.

Add Carico purified water, spices and tomatoes, mix well, reduce the heat to low and simmer, uncovered, 45 minutes to 1 hour or until reduced by about one-third.

NUTRITIONAL BREAKDOWN PER SERVING: Calories 73; Fat Grams 3; Carbohydrate Grams 9; Protein Grams 1; Cholesterol mg 0; Sodium mg 330.

How to Peel & Seed Tomatoes

Equipment: 2 large mixing bowls, 5-quart (4.7 L) roaster/saucepan, paring knife, slotted serving spoon, 8 or 10-inch chef knife

In a mixing bowl, prepare an ice bath of ice and Carico purified water. Add ice as needed to stay cold.

Fill the 5-quart (4.7 L) roaster/saucepan halfway with Carico purified water and bring to a boil over medium-high heat. With a paring knife cut out the core stem, and score an X across the bottom of the tomatoes. Using a slotted spoon with long handle, place tomatoes in boiling water, 2 to 3 minutes, or until the skin at the X begins to peel back slightly. Using the slotted spoon, quickly remove tomatoes to ice bath.

Using the paring knife, begin at the X to peel the skin from the tomato. With a chef knife, slice the tomato in half and scoop out the seeds with a tablespoon.

Plum tomatoes peeled and seeded can be used in a variety of tomato based recipes.

Rosemary Potatoes

Serves: 8
Preparation Time: 1 hour 10 minutes
Equipment: 8 or 10-inch chef knife, cutting board, 5-quart (4.7 L) covered
roaster/saucepan

1	tablespoon olive oil
1	tablespoon unsalted butter
1	tablespoon fresh rosemary, chopped
1	teaspoon fresh thyme, chopped
½	red bell pepper, cubed
½	onion, chopped
4	large baking potatoes, about ¼ pound each, cut into 1-inch cubes
1	tablespoon fresh parsley, chopped

In the 5-quart (4.7 L) roaster/saucepan, melt butter in olive oil over medium to medium-high heat. Add all ingredients and toss to coat. Cover, open the Ultra-Temp™ control and whistle valve. When the whistle sounds, close the Ultra-Temp™ control and whistle valve. Reduce to medium-low heat and spin the cover to form the Ultra-Seal™. Begin timing, cook for 30 to 35 minutes. The optimum cooking temperature for root vegetables (potatoes, carrots, turnips, etc.) is when the temperature gauge registers between 160-195°F (71-91°C).

To serve, spoon into serving bowl, gently toss and top with chopped parsley.

NUTRITIONAL BREAKDOWN PER SERVING: Calories 150; Fat Grams 3; Carbohydrate Grams 28; Protein Grams 3; Cholesterol mg 4; Sodium mg 24.

Warm Green Bean Salad

Serves: 4
Preparation Time: 25 minutes
Equipment: paring knife, chef knife, cutting board, 1.7-quart (1.6 L)
covered saucepan/skillet, small mixing bowl

1	pound fresh green beans, trimmed
3	tablespoons red wine vinegar
2	tablespoons fresh oregano, chopped or 1 tablespoon dried
1	tablespoon Dijon mustard
2	cloves garlic, minced
1	teaspoon olive oil (optional)
¼	teaspoon freshly ground black pepper

Fill the pan with green beans, rinse with Carico purified water and pour the excess water off. The water that clings to the green beans is sufficient for cooking the waterless way. Cover the pan, open the Ultra-Temp™ control and whistle valve and cook over medium heat. When the whistle sounds, close the Ultra-Temp™ control and whistle valve, reduce to low-heat and spin the cover to form the vapor seal. Cook 10 to 15 minutes. Don't peek. Removing the cover will destroy the Ultra-Seal™ and lengthen the cooking time.

While the green beans are cooking, combine the vinegar, oregano, mustard, garlic and olive oil, if using, in a small mixing bowl. Mix well and set aside.

Remove the green beans from the heat and drain the excess moisture from the pan. Add the dressing to the pan and stir gently. Cover the pan and let stand for 5 minutes, or until dressing is warmed.

To serve, toss the green beans to combine all the ingredients. Sprinkle with pepper and serve warm.

NUTRITIONAL BREAKDOWN PER SERVING: Calories 36; Fat Grams 0.3; Carbohydrate Grams 8.2; Protein Grams 2; Cholesterol mg 0; Sodium mg 43. (Olive oil adds 8 Calories and 1g Fat per serving.)

Cabbage Casserole

Serves: 4 to 6

Preparation Time: 20 minutes

Equipment: 8 or 10-inch chef knife, cutting board, 3-quart (2.8 L) covered saucepan

1	medium onion, diced
1	clove garlic, minced
¼	pound ground turkey
½	teaspoon fresh thyme, chopped or ¼ teaspoon dried thyme
½	teaspoon fresh oregano, chopped or ¼ teaspoon dried oregano
½	cup seeded, diced plum tomatoes or canned whole
1	teaspoon sugar
1	teaspoon white distilled vinegar
1	bay leaf
½	cup cooked rice
½	head green cabbage, shredded
2	teaspoons chopped fresh parsley

In a hot, dry 3-quart (2.8 L) saucepan over medium heat, dry sauté the onion and garlic until lightly browned, about 5 minutes, stirring occasionally.

Add the ground turkey, stirring to break up until cooked through, about 5 minutes. Stir in the thyme, oregano, tomatoes, sugar, vinegar, bay leaf and rice. Rinse the shredded cabbage in Carico purified water and add it to the pan. The pan must be at least three-quarters full for the Ultra-Seal™ to form. Cover the pan and open the Ultra-Temp™ control and whistle valve. When the whistle sounds, close the whistle valve, reduce the heat to low and spin the cover to form the Ultra-Seal™. Cook for 10 to 15 minutes. Don't peek. Removing the cover will destroy the Ultra-Seal™ and lengthen the cooking time. The Ultra-Temp™ temperature gauge should read directly between 160-195°F (71-91°C) to cook the waterless way.

To serve, discard the bay leaf and sprinkle with parsley.

NUTRITIONAL BREAKDOWN PER SERVING: Calories 69; Fat Grams 1.8; Carbohydrate Grams 9; Protein Grams 4.8; Cholesterol mg 15; Sodium mg 125.

French Tarragon Potatoes

Serves: 4 to 6
Preparation Time: 30 minutes
Equipment: paring knife, 3-quart (2.8 L) covered saucepan, mixing bowl

12	small red potatoes, cut in half
1	tablespoon red wine vinegar
1	tablespoon Dijon mustard
3	tablespoons sour cream
1	tablespoon minced fresh tarragon
½	teaspoon freshly ground black pepper

Scrub the potatoes with a vegetable brush, remove surface blemishes with a paring knife and place in 3-quart (2.8 L) saucepan. Do not peel. Fill the pan with Carico purified water and allow to soak 5 to 10 minutes.

Drain and rinse with Carico purified water. Pour most of the water off. The water that clings to the potatoes is sufficient for waterless cooking.

Cover the pan with the Ultra-Temp™ control with whistle valve open and place the pan over medium heat. When the whistle sounds the temperature gauge should register between 160-195°F (71-91°C), in the center of the cooking range of the thermometer. Close the whistle valve, reduce the heat to low and spin the cover to form a vapor seal (Ultra-Seal™). Cook for 15 to 20 minutes per quart.

While the potatoes are cooking, combine the vinegar, mustard, sour cream and fresh tarragon in a mixing bowl. Mix well and set aside.

To serve, top the potatoes with the sour cream dressing and sprinkle with pepper.

NUTRITIONAL BREAKDOWN PER SERVING: Calories 189; Fat Grams 1.3; Carbohydrate Grams 40; Protein Grams 4.9; Cholesterol mg 2; Sodium mg 27.

Pan Roasted Potatoes

Serves: 4 to 6
Preparation Time: 25 minutes
Equipment: paring knife, 8-inch chef knife, 11-inch covered fry/sauté
skillet, Carico pierced turner

4	medium russet potatoes
½	teaspoon olive oil
¼	teaspoon garlic powder
¼	teaspoon sweet paprika
1	teaspoon chopped fresh parsley

Fill the 11-inch fry/sauté skillet half full with Carico purified water, scrub the potatoes with a vegetable brush and remove surface blemishes with a paring knife. Do not peel. Cut the potatoes in quarters with the chef knife. Soak in Carico purified water for 10 to 15 minutes, then pat dry with a paper towel.

Place the potatoes, flesh side down, in a hot, dry skillet over medium heat. Cover the pan and close the Ultra-Temp™ control and whistle valve. The potatoes will stick at first; when finished browning, they will release easily from the pan. Using a Carico pierced turner, turn the potatoes and brown on all sides, 6 to 7 minutes per side. Cover after each turning.

To serve, brush the potatoes with olive oil and sprinkle with garlic powder, paprika and parsley.

NUTRITIONAL BREAKDOWN PER SERVING: Calories 72; Fat Grams 0.1; Carbohydrate Grams 16; Protein Grams 1.9; Cholesterol mg 0; Sodium mg 6.

Yellow Squash Southern Style

Serves: 6 to 8
Preparation Time: 30 minutes
Equipment: 8 to 10-inch chef knife, 2-quart (1.9 L) covered saucepan, 9-inch gourmet skillet, masher, stainless steel cake pan

6	medium summer squash, diced
½	medium onion, diced
1	tablespoon sugar
¼	teaspoon white pepper
¾	cup dry Italian bread crumbs
1	teaspoon chopped fresh parsley
½	medium lemon, quartered

Fill the 2-quart (1.9 L) saucepan with summer squash. Rinse with Carico purified water and pour most of the water off. The water that clings to the squash is sufficient for waterless cooking. Cover the pan, open the Ultra-Temp™ control and whistle valve, and place over medium heat. When the whistle sounds the temperature gauge should register between 160-195°F (71-91°C), in the center of the cooking range of the thermometer. Close the whistle valve, reduce the heat to low and spin the cover to create a vapor seal (Ultra-Seal™). Cook 5 to 6 minutes. Turn the heat off and set aside.

In a hot, dry gourmet skillet, dry sauté the onion over medium heat until slightly browned, about 5 minutes, stirring occasionally. Remove from the heat.

Drain the excess moisture off the squash. With the masher, coarsely mash the squash. Add the onion, sugar and pepper; mix well.

Place the mixture in a Carico stainless steel cake pan. Top with bread crumbs and place under a preheated broiler for 3 to 5 minutes. With a potholder, remove the cake pan to a trivet.

To serve, sprinkle with parsley and serve with lemon wedges.

NUTRITIONAL BREAKDOWN PER SERVING: Calories 69; Fat Grams 0.9; Carbohydrate Grams 14; Protein Grams 2.4; Cholesterol mg 0; Sodium mg 107.

Punjabi Potatoes with Cauliflower

Serves: 4
Preparation Time: 35 minutes
Equipment: paring knife, 3-quart (2.8 L) covered saucepan, 1.7-quart (1.6 L) covered saucepan, 8 or 10-inch chef knife, large mixing bowl

4	medium red potatoes
1	medium onion, diced
1	teaspoon grated fresh ginger
½	cup diced, seeded plum tomatoes or canned tomatoes
3	tablespoons curry powder
½	head of cauliflower, broken into florets
2	tablespoons Chardonnay wine or Carico purified water
1	teaspoon chopped fresh parsley

Fill the 3-quart (2.8 L) saucepan with Carico purified water, scrub the potatoes with a vegetable brush and remove surface blemishes with a paring knife. Do not peel. Return the potatoes to the pan to soak for 15 minutes.

In a hot, dry 1.7-quart (1.6 L) saucepan over medium heat, dry sauté the onion until slightly browned, about 5 minutes, stirring occasionally. Stir in the ginger, tomatoes and curry powder and sauté 2 to 3 minutes. Remove from heat and allow to cool slightly.

Drain the potatoes, add the cauliflower and rinse again with Carico purified water. Pour the water off, cover, open the Ultra-Temp™ control and whistle valve and place over medium heat. When the whistle sounds the temperature gauge should register between 160-195°F (71-91°C), in the center of the cooking range of the thermometer. Close the whistle valve, reduce the heat to low and spin the cover to create a vapor seal (Ultra-Seal™). Begin timing; cook 25 to 30 minutes. Don't peek. Removing the cover will destroy the Ultra-Seal™, lengthen the cooking time and may cause the potatoes to burn.

To serve, top with the tomato-ginger curry sauce and sprinkle with parsley.

NUTRITIONAL BREAKDOWN PER SERVING: Calories 102; Fat Grams 0.8; Carbohydrate Grams 22; Protein Grams 3.2; Cholesterol mg 0; Sodium mg 125.

Salsa de Pomodoro

Spaghetti Sauce
Makes: 20 to 24 cups
Preparation Time: 3½ hours
Equipment: 8 or 10-inch chef knife, 12-quart (11.4 L) covered stockpot

2	large onions, diced
6	cloves garlic, minced
3	tablespoons Italian seasoning
2	5.5 ounce cans tomato paste
½	cup Chianti or other dry red wine
3	28 ounce cans whole tomatoes
3	28 ounce cans tomato puree
10	cups Carico purified water
¼	cup sugar

In a hot, dry 12-quart (11.4 L) stockpot, over medium heat, dry sauté the onions and garlic until slightly browned, about 5 minutes, stirring occasionally. If you prefer, add 1 to 2 tablespoons olive oil.

Stir in the Italian seasoning and allow it to release its flavor. Add the tomato paste and cook, stirring until the paste turns a reddish-brown color, 5 to 7 minutes. Do not allow the residue that forms on the bottom of the pan to burn.

Deglaze the pan with the wine. Add the tomatoes, tomato puree, water and sugar. Stir, cover the pan, open the Ultra-Temp™ control and whistle valve and reduce to medium-low heat. Simmer 2 to 3 hours, stirring occasionally.

NUTRITIONAL BREAKDOWN PER ½ CUP: Calories 41; Fat Grams 0.03; Carbohydrate Grams 9.4; Protein Grams 1.5; Cholesterol mg 0; Sodium mg 42.

Mom's Famous Potato Salad

Serves: 12
Preparation Time: 1 hour 30 minutes
Equipment: paring knife, 3-quart (2.8 L) covered saucepan, 8 or 10-inch
chef knife, large mixing bowl

6-8	medium potatoes
½	green bell pepper, seeded and diced
1	medium onion, diced
3	medium radishes, diced
1	stalk celery, diced
4	sweet pickles, diced
2	tablespoons pickle juice
½	cup mayonnaise
1	tablespoon sugar
1	tablespoon apple cider vinegar or white distilled
4	hard boiled eggs, sliced (optional)

Fill the 3-quart (2.8 L) saucepan with Carico purified water, scrub the potatoes with a vegetable brush and remove surface blemishes with a paring knife. Do not peel. Return to pan to soak for 15 minutes.

Drain the potatoes, rinse again with Carico purified water and pour most of the water off. Cover the pan, open the Ultra-Temp™ control and whistle valve and place over medium heat. When the whistle sounds the temperature gauge should register between 160-195°F (71-91°C), in the center of the cooking range of the thermometer. Close the whistle valve and reduce the heat to low. Spin the cover to create the vapor seal (Ultra-Seal™). Begin timing. Cook 25 to 30 minutes after forming the seal. Don't peek. Removing the cover will destroy the Ultra-Seal™, lengthen the cooking time and may cause the potatoes to burn.

Test the potatoes for doneness. If not done, cover the pan, close the Ultra-Temp™ control and whistle valve and add 2 tablespoons of Carico purified water to the rim to reestablish the Ultra-Seal™. Cook over low heat for 5 to 10 minutes. Remove from heat and set aside.

While the potatoes are cooling, combine the remaining ingredients in the mixing bowl. When the potatoes have cooled sufficiently, cut in ½-inch cubes, add to the mixing bowl and stir gently. Cover and refrigerate for about 1 hour. For a more intense flavor, cover with the small Ultra-Vac lid, pump the air out and refrigerate for up to 24 hours.

To serve, spoon into serving bowl and garnish with sliced eggs.

NUTRITIONAL BREAKDOWN PER SERVING: Calories 76; Fat Grams 3.7; Carbohydrate Grams 10; Protein Grams 1; Cholesterol mg 3; Sodium mg 125.

CHAPTER 11

Top of the Range Baking

Ultra-Tech II™ is designed to bake cakes, cornbread, cookies, casseroles, meatloaf, ribs and lasagna in the pan, on top of the range, more efficiently than in the oven. For example, to bake a small cake, preheat a 1.7-quart (1.6 L) or 3-quart (2.8 L) saucepan over medium heat. Melt unsalted butter (or coat with non-stick cooking spray). Pour the cake batter into the pan until the pan is half full, cover and open the Ultra-Temp™ control and whistle valve. When the whistle sounds, reduce the heat to low and finish baking (about 12 to 15 minutes). When using this method, foods with crust toppings, as well as pies and some breads, will not brown.

NOTE: Higher altitudes may require longer baking times.

Marbled Brownies

Yields: 2 dozen
Preparation Time: 30 minutes
Equipment: 2 mixing bowls, electric mixer, 11-inch covered fry/sauté skillet

4	tablespoons unsalted butter, softened
½	cup cream cheese, softened
½	cup sugar
2	eggs, beaten, or 4 egg whites
1	teaspoon natural vanilla bean, or vanilla extract
¾	cup organic whole wheat flour, or rice flour
½	teaspoon baking powder
1	pinch kosher salt
3	tablespoons unsweetened cocoa

In the mixing bowl, cream butter and cream cheese together. Gradually add sugar, beating at medium speed with an electric mixer until light and fluffy. Add eggs and vanilla, beating well.

In a separate mixing bowl, combine flour, baking powder and a pinch of salt; add to butter/cream cheese mixture, beating well. Divide batter into 2 separate mixing bowls; sift cocoa over half of batter and fold in gently.

Spoon the cocoa batter into the 11-inch fry/sauté skillet. Pour remaining half vanilla batter over cocoa batter. Gently cut through batter with a butter knife to create a swirling marble effect. Cover, close the Ultra-Temp™ control and whistle valve, bake on top of the stove over medium-low heat for 20 minutes. The thermometer should register between 160-195°F (71-91°C), in the center of the cooking range of the temperature gauge. Test with toothpick.

To serve, allow brownies to cool, then cut into 2-inch squares.

NUTRITIONAL BREAKDOWN PER SERVING: Calories 57; Fat Grams 2; Carbohydrate Grams 9; Protein Grams 1; Cholesterol mg 2; Sodium mg 74.

Chocolate Glazed Poached Pears

Serves: 6

Preparation Time: 45 minutes

Equipment: 6-quart (5.7 L) covered roaster/saucepan, stainless steel cookie sheet, 3-quart (2.8 L) covered saucepan, double boiler

6	firm but ripe pears
3	tablespoons Carico purified water, or Chardonnay wine
3	ounces sweet dark chocolate, chopped
3	ounces semisweet dark chocolate, chopped
¼	cup unsalted butter
	Springs of mint for garnish

Although we do not recommend peeling, if skin is thick, peel pears using a vegetable peeler, leaving stems intact. If necessary, cut a small slice off each pear's bottom so it will stand upright in the pan.

Stand pears in Carico purified water (or wine) in the 6-quart (5.7 L) roaster/saucepan, cover the pan, open the Ultra-Temp™ control and whistle valve and place over medium heat. When the whistle sounds the temperature gauge should register between 160-195°F (71-91°C), in the center of the cooking range of the temperature gauge. Close the whistle valve, reduce the heat to low and spin the cover to create a vapor seal (Ultra-Seal™). Begin timing, cook 15 to 20 minutes. Don't peek. Removing the cover will destroy the Ultra-Seal™, lengthen the cooking time and may cause the pears to burn.

Remove pears with a slotted spoon and place on cookie sheet to cool. Pears may be refrigerated several hours (or overnight) if desired in the roaster/saucepan using the large Carico Ultra-Vac™ cover.

GLAZE

Several hours before serving, melt both varieties of chocolate and butter in the Carico double boiler, over simmering water, at medium-low heat, stirring occasionally. When smooth, remove from heat.

NOTE: If melting chocolate on an induction cooktop, chocolate renders best at 110°F (43°C).

Blot all pears dry with paper towels, and line cookie sheet with wax paper. Holding each pear carefully by the stem, dip into the chocolate glazing mixture, tilting pear and spooning glaze to cover completely. Place on cookie sheet and refrigerate for several hours. Before serving, remove pears to serving plate with spatula, and garnish with mint.

NUTRITIONAL BREAKDOWN PER SERVING: Calories 292; Fat Grams 7; Carbohydrate Grams 45; Protein Grams 13; Cholesterol mg 69; Sodium mg 140.

Angel Food Cake

Serves: 8-10

Preparation Time: 2 hours

Equipment: electric mixer, mixing bowls, 6-quart (5.7 L) roaster/saucepan, large high-dome cover, 9-inch gourmet skillet

1¼ cups egg whites (approximately 7 large eggs)
1 teaspoon cream of tartar
2 tablespoons Carico purified water
1½ cups sugar
½ teaspoon vanilla extract
½ teaspoon almond extract
1 cup cake flour, sifted twice

With the electric mixer, beat egg whites in a large mixing bowl at high speed until frothy, about 1 minute. Add cream of tartar, and beat 3 minutes. Add water and continue beating at high speed until whites stand at peaks, about 3 to 4 minutes. Turn mixer to low speed; add sugar gradually, then add vanilla and almond extracts. Beat about ½ minute longer. Fold sifted flour in by hand.

Coat 6-quart (5.7 L) roaster/saucepan with unsalted butter. Place greased angel food cake tube (or tall heavy glass) in center of 6-quart saucepan and pour batter into pan. Cover with large dome cover, bake over medium-low heat for 45 to 50 minutes. To cool, place on wire rack for 1 hour, then loosen with knife around edges and gently remove cake. Lightly brush off crumbs.

DON'T PEEK! LIFTING THE COVER WILL CAUSE CAKE TO FALL. Cake top will cook dry but not brown.

To serve, slice and top with fresh berries.

NUTRITIONAL BREAKDOWN PER SERVING: Calories 150; Fat Grams 0; Carbohydrate Grams 34; Protein Grams 0; Cholesterol mg 0; Sodium 51.

ABOUT THE AUTHOR

Chef Charles Knight traces his culinary roots to his childhood and the home kitchens of the diverse ethnic neighborhoods of his hometown, Rahway, New Jersey. His love for cooking and recipes began with earning a Cooking Merit Badge with Cub Scout Pack 47. While still in high school, he worked in butcher shops, restaurants and industrial kitchens throughout northern New Jersey.

His most inspirational culinary studies came from working with his former business partner and TV personality, Chef Tell. Later in life, he earned a formal culinary education attending Institute of Culinary Education in New York City, and earned credits in Nutritional Cuisine from the Culinary Institute of America in Hyde Park, New York.

Chef Knight is a bestselling cookbook author, former Restaurateur, Radio and TV cooking show host, cookware designer, and is recognized worldwide as the foremost expert on the classic methods of waterless/greaseless cooking.

Food Editor, Contributor: **Lois Smith,** also born and raised in Rahway, NJ, was introduced to Charles Knight by her husband, Scott Smith, a fellow Rahway High School classmate of Charles. Lois spent 33 years working for the pharmaceutical manufacturer, Merck & Co., Inc. in various roles within their International Division, while completing coursework at Seton Hall University and Kean University in New Jersey. Lois loves to cook and appreciates the benefits of healthy eating. Now the proud owner of a complete set of Carico cookware, she is enjoying waterless and greaseless cooking at her new home in Charleston, South Carolina.

NOTES:

97185361R00069

Made in the USA
Columbia, SC
11 June 2018